An Illustrated History of Texas Forts

Rod Timanus

Republic of Texas Press
Plano, Texas

HOUSTON PUBLIC LIBRARY

R01278 75798

itxry

Library of Congress Cataloging-in-Publication Data

Timanus, Rod
   An illustrated history of Texas forts / Rod Timanus.
      p. cm.
   Includes bibliographical references and index.
   ISBN 1-55622-795-7 (pbk.)
   1. Fortification--Texas--Guidebooks. 2. Texas--Guidebooks. I. Title.

UG411.T4 T55   2000
355.7'09764--dc21   00-045825
                                                          CIP

Friends of the © 2001, Rod Timanus
Houston Public Library All Rights Reserved

Republic of Texas Press is an imprint of Wordware Publishing, Inc.
No part of this book may be reproduced in any form or by
any means without permission in writing from
Wordware Publishing, Inc.

Printed in the United States of America

ISBN 1-55622-795-7
10 9 8 7 6 5 4 3 2 1
0011

All inquiries for volume purchases of this book should be addressed to Wordware Publishing, Inc., at 2320 Los Rios Boulevard, Plano, Texas 75074. Telephone inquiries may be made by calling:
(972) 423-0090

Dedication

Dedicated to the memory of my late father, William Stevens Timanus, and my late brother, Bryan Stevens Timanus, who both loved this country and its history.

Contents

Preface ix
Acknowledgment xi

Spanish Presidio Period 1
   Typical Spanish Presidio 2
   Fort St. Louis 4
   Mission San Antonio de Valero 7
      Fortress Alamo 10
      Battles of the Alamo 11
   Presidio San Antonio de Bexar 20
   Presidio Nuestra Señora de Loreto 23
      Presidio La Bahia 23
      Fort Goliad 26
      Fort Defiance 28
   Fuerte de Santa Cruz del Cibolo 34
   Presidio San Elizario 35
   The Y'Barbo House 36
   The Stone Fort 37
   East Tejas Presidios 41
   Presidio San Luis de las Amarillas 45
   Real Presidio de San Saba 47

Mexico & Texas Revolution Period 51
   Fort Anahuac 52
   Fort Velasco 57
   Fort Lipantitlan 61
   Fort Tenoxtitlan 64
   Fort Teran 66
   Fort Bend 66
   Fort Parker 68
   Fort Lacy 71
   Tumlinson Fort 72
   Fort Houston 72

Contents

    Fort Milam 73

Republic of Texas Period 75
    Typical Family Fort 76
    Fort Lyday 77
    Fort Oldham 78
    Fort Fisher 78
    Adobe Walls 81
        First Battle of Adobe Walls 83
        Second Battle of Adobe Walls 84
    Fort Bird 87
    Fort Travis 88
    Camp Bowie 88
    Camp Crockett 89
    Camp Chambers 89
    Fort Sherman 89
    Little River Fort 90
    Fort Burleson 90
    Fort Colorado 93

Mexican War Period 95
    Fort Marcy 96
    Fort Texas 97
    Fort Brown 100
    Fort Polk 103

U.S. Army Period (1848-1861) 105
    Typical U.S. Army fort 106
    Fort Graham 108
    Fort Lincoln 108
    Fort Gates 108
    Fort Merrill 109
    Fort Terrett 109
    Camp Wood 109
    Buffalo Springs 109
    Camp Pena Colorado 110
    Fort Ewell 110

Fort Hancock 110
Fort Martin Scott 112
Fort Ringgold 114
Fort Leaton 117
Fort Bliss 120
Fort Worth 125
Fort Croghan 126
Fort Duncan 128
Fort McIntosh 131
Fort Inge 135
Fort Belknap 137
Fort Phantom Hill 141
Fort Mason 144
Fort Clark 146
Fort Chadbourne 150
Fort McKavett 151
Fort Picketville 154
Fort Davis 154
Camp Verde 160
Fort Lancaster 162
Camp Cooper 163
Fort Hudson 164
Fort Cibolo 166
Fort Stockton 170
Fort Quitman 175

Confederate Period ***177***
    Camp Breckenridge 178
    Camp Collier 178
    Camp Cureton 178
    Camp Dix 179
    Camp McMillan 179
    Camp Montel 179
    Camp Nueces 179
    Camp Pecan 179
    Camp Rabb 180

Contents

　　Red River Station. 180
　　Camp Salmon. 180
　　Camp San Saba. 180
　　Camp Verde. 180
　　Camp Llano and Camp Davis. 180
　　Blair's Fort 181
　　Camp Ford 182
　　Fort Waul. 185
　　Davis Family Fort 187
　　Fort Sabine 189
　　Buffalo Springs. 190
　　Fort Griffin 191
　　Fort Grigsby 195
　　Fort Manhassett 195
　　Camp Semmes 196
　　Fort Quintana. 196
　　Fort Esperanza 197
　　Fort Green 198

U.S. Army Period (1866-Present). **201**
　　Fort Richardson. 202
　　Fort Concho 205
　　Fort Griffin 209
　　Fort Elliott 212
　　Fort Sam Houston 213
　　Camp Mabry 218
　　Fort Crockett 220
　　Fort San Jacinto 221
　　Fort D.A. Russell 222
　　Fort Hood. 223

Bibliography. 225
Index. 229

Preface

"A strong or fortified place."

Most modern dictionaries will begin the definition of the word "fort" with that description. That one phrase would be quite familiar to the eighteenth- and nineteenth-century inhabitants of Texas, since their very survival often depended upon occupying such a place as protection from their enemies. As a northern province of Mexico, an independent Republic, and finally as a State of both the Union and the Confederacy, Texas was contested ground for much of its early history. The Mexicans fought the Spanish for control of Texas; the Anglos fought the Mexicans for possession of Texas and then fought each other. The Native Americans fought everybody. In each conflict, whether short and savage in duration or protracted and bloody, one faction or the other often fought from "a strong or fortified place."

Throughout the history of Texas there have been forts constructed. Many were never needed and eventually abandoned to disappear from sight and memory. Others saw much use and were recorded in the annals of history, never to fade from mind. Still others were not intended for use as forts but were converted to that purpose as needs arose, the Alamo in San Antonio and the Stone Fort in Nacogdoches being prime examples. The former was a Franciscan mission complex and the latter a private residence. Both were strong places that served the necessity to "fort up" against hostile forces.

In the following pages I have attempted to provide a list of Texas forts in chronological order. That is, in the order they came into being and not necessarily when they became famous, or infamous, in Texas history. For example the notations for the Alamo and Presidio La Bahia (Fort Defiance at

Preface

Goliad) will not be found in the Texas Revolution section but in the Spanish Presidio section. These two places, to be sure, derive their fame from the Texas Revolution, but they were already ancient when that conflict commenced.

Also, in some instances a fort, or any trace of it, does not exist today. I was then faced with the task of deciding whether or not to include a notation in this book. I based my decision on many factors, the primary being how a fort fit into a specific historical context. Just because a particular fort may be excluded does not mean that I did not know about it, but rather I chose not to include it in the text. Sit down at a computer, go to the *Handbook of Texas Online*, type in the keyword "Presidio," and you will understand my dilemma. There are 581 notations listed.

Graphically, my illustrations are based upon written descriptions, period drawings, plans, and maps. There is some, but not much, conjecture on my part as to how things might have looked, sometimes referred to as artistic license, and much on-site observation. The results, I believe, provide as factual a viewing experience as possible.

Here then, in words and pictures, is a history of the forts of Texas.

Acknowledgment

This book began with a telephone call from my good friend Bill Groneman in 1999. I have had the great honor of working with him in the past, creating maps and graphics for several of his books. He phoned to tell me he had recommended me to Republic of Texas Press as just the right person to tackle this project. Of course, I jumped at the opportunity, and the end result you now hold in your hands. If, when you finish reading this book, you are pleased with my efforts, then I have succeeded in what I set out to accomplish. On the other hand, if you are disappointed, then please remember this was Bill's idea...

All kidding aside, the creation of this book has been a strange and wonderful experience full of frustrations and triumphs. It has been an odyssey of countless hours poring over reams of printed material and of staring into a computer monitor late into the night gathering online information. It's been the experience of having my daughter's puppy shred and eat a quarter of my handwritten notes, really, and of typing and drawing until my fingers were sore. All the time I wondered why any sane person would want to do this for a living. But compared to the hardships and danger the people I've written about in this book endured, my journey to this point has been as pleasant as a stroll on the River Walk in San Antonio. Many people helped me out along the way, and I must take a moment to thank them for their support.

First and foremost, my daughter Rebecca, who unselfishly guarded and maintained our home-fort while I drove to Texas for some on-site research. The lovely Terry LaPlante, who graciously allowed me the use of her quiet, secluded home to gather my thoughts and write and draw far removed from

Acknowledgment

everyday distractions. She also rode herd on me and kept me focused on my task with her interest and encouragement. Fellow Alamo Society member Jeffrey Dane, always ready with a kind word and a trivia question online, bolstered my sagging spirits at crucial times. My editor, Ginnie Bivona, guided me through the process of creating this book with grace and good humor. Martha McCuller provided invaluable technical assistance during the publication process. The Western Writers of America welcomed me into their organization without qualification, even though I was an "easterner," and I have made many friends there and learned much from them about the business of writing. Bill and Kelly Groneman have always been there for me with words of advice, and I'm pleased to have them as friends. I have to mention Mr. Bobby Balser of Balser's Northside Automotive in Kerrville, Texas, for kindly making time to do repairs on my truck so I could continue my research trip, because I told him I would do so.

The support of my family has always been important. My mother, Marjorie Timanus, my sister, Anne Hoskins, who helped supply me with much research material, my brother-in-law, Howard Hoskins (a bona fide Texan), and my nieces, Heather and Amanda, have been a source of strength and inspiration throughout this endeavor. My aunt, Florence Mahoney (Aunt Mimi), and my cousins, Maree Gregoire and Martha Miller and their families, also sustained me with their interest and well wishes. I hope I've made them proud.

All that said, I think it's time to head to Texas, and I think you'll enjoy the trip. I know I did.

Spanish Presidio Period

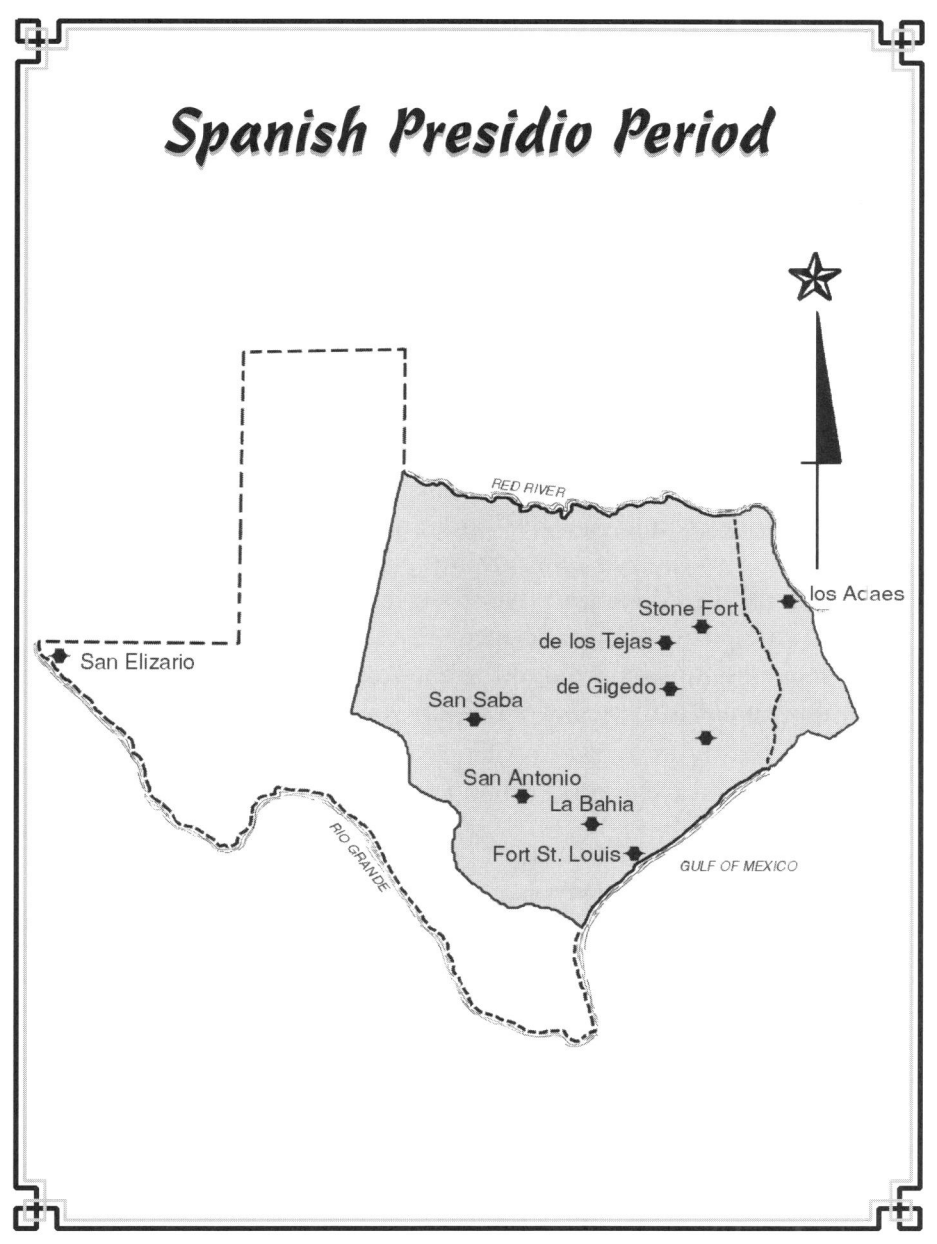

Typical Spanish Presidio

Unlike the U.S. Army, which would follow a century later, the Spanish believed in walls. Their presidios, forts, were enclosed, self-sustaining communities designed to provide protection from hostile Indians. Walls kept the garrison in—many times nothing more than convicts serving their sentences in the military instead of prison—and the enemy out. Rarely was a military campaign mounted against the Indians; though there were retaliation raids, a more defensive posture was preferred.

A presidio was encircled by walls of wood or stone, by official mandate, and usually contained houses for officers, soldiers, and their families. Many presidios had a chapel so the garrison could attend their own services instead of traveling to a nearby mission. In most cases the presidio was built near a mission and charged with protecting the friars and Indian converts there as well as any local settlers.

Typically, the layout of the presidio was roughly square, with buildings along the inside of the walls, forming a central plaza. At each corner there was supposed to be a raised bastion for the placement of protective cannons. This was not always the case, as local building materials dictated, but every effort was made to comply with the standard construction regulations. The mandated garrison size of fifty officers and men was rarely, if ever, fully met, and this caused a few shortcuts and changes in building styles as manpower shortages made them necessary. As a result, some presidios were large and expansive while others were no bigger than a large house.

The northern province of Tejas was never fully settled or protected by the Spanish, other than small enclaves of ranchers, farmers, and the mission sites. By and large, the Indians held free reign over their territory and were unchallenged. But the Spanish, and later Mexican, presence took firm root in many areas, due in large part to the establishment of the isolated presidios on the frontier.

French explorer Rene Robert Cavelier Sieur de LaSalle left Canada in 1682 and sailed down the entire length of the Mississippi River. Arriving at the Gulf of Mexico, he claimed all the lands he had traveled through for France and named the area Louisiana. His claim, stretching from French Canada to the Gulf of Mexico, cut Spanish Tejas off from Spanish Florida and froze the British in place along the eastern coast of the North American continent. Returning to Canada and then to France, he set plans in motion to return to the Gulf coast with French colonists.

Fort St. Louis

In 1685, with three ships loaded with settlers and supplies, the LaSalle expedition sailed into the Gulf of Mexico. One other ship, the *St. Francois*, had been lost en route to the Spanish navy in the Caribbean. But, proving that even intrepid explorers can lose their way, he sailed right past his destination of the mouth of the Mississippi River. One month and 400 miles too far west he realized his mistake and prepared to turn back eastward. One of his ships, the *Aimable*, was wrecked on shoals at the entrance to Matagorda Bay on the Tejas coast. Another ship, the *Joly*, its crew and passengers thoroughly terrified and angry at LaSalle's error, simply sailed away with the intention of returning to France. LaSalle managed to get his remaining ship, the *Belle*, past the shoals safely and into Matagorda Bay. He began landing his people on the shore and, not realizing just where he was, claimed this new land in the name of France.

Moving inland, LaSalle supervised the construction of a wooden stockade overlooking Garcitas Creek, which he christened Fort St. Louis. The stockade surrounded one large and six small log cabins that housed the remaining Frenchmen.

LaSalle explored the surrounding countryside while the *Belle* sailed and charted the waters of the bay. At one point LaSalle even came upon the Brazos River and mistook it for the Mississippi. Continuing strife with the local Karankawa Indians forced the French to curtail activities outside the fort until they were virtual prisoners within the stockade. A year passed as the climate, Indians, poisonous snakes, sickness, accidents, and even alligators killed off the French at an alarming rate. By 1686 there were only forty-four settlers left at Fort St. Louis when the final blow fell. LaSalle's last ship, the *Belle*, sank.

His only link to the outside world now at the bottom of the bay, LaSalle began to seriously consider mounting an expedition that would have to walk to Canada to get help for the faltering colony. In January of 1687, leaving behind the women and children and those men too ill to walk, LaSalle led most of the remaining able-bodied men out of the fort and started his journey. He moved east, hoping to at last find the Mississippi River and follow it north. Gabriel Minime Sieur Barbier was left in charge of Fort St. Louis. Smallpox broke out in the fort shortly after LaSalle's departure.

By March, hatred for their haughty and hard-driving leader reached the breaking point among some of the men marching with LaSalle. Somewhere in east Tejas, they shot and killed him from ambush. Those still loyal to LaSalle managed to escape and eventually, incredibly, succeeded in making their way to Canada. At the same time at Fort St. Louis, Barbier realized that a truce with the Karankawa would allow the French more freedom of movement outside the walls and perhaps help aid in the recovery of those ravaged by disease. When a group of Indians were spotted lurking nearby, Barbier threw open the gates as an invitation to come in and make friends. Armed warriors raced into the fort and massacred most of the inhabitants, carrying off some women and children.

The Spanish, meanwhile, had gotten word of the French "invasion" of their territory and in 1689 sent a military expedition to locate and expel the intruders. When they found Fort St. Louis it was a looted, crumbling shell, its eight naval cannons standing silent guard against an enemy who had already won. Searching the surrounding countryside for survivors and finding only two men, two boys, and a woman among the local Indian tribes, the Spanish burned what remained of the fort and marched away.

A French rescue mission finally sailed into Matagorda Bay in 1690, but there was no trace of Fort St. Louis or its colonists. Any evidence of the fort was probably wiped out in 1721 when the Spanish constructed the Presidio Nuestra Señora Santa Maria de Loreto de la Bahia del Espiritu Santo on the site.

Later History

In the late 1940s archeological studies located the site of Fort St. Louis. In 1995 the sunken wreck of the *Belle* was discovered in Matagorda Bay and salvaged. Today a historical marker stands at the intersection of FM 444 and U.S. 59, thirteen miles southeast of the city of Inez, to mark the location of the doomed French fort.

The Spanish mission of San Antonio de Valero is not remembered as the first of five missions built in the Tejas province town of San Antonio de Bexar. It is not remembered for the murmured prayers of priests as they sought to convert the local Native Americans to civilization and Christianity. It is remembered as The Alamo, and its history is recorded in fire and blood.

Mission San Antonio de Valero

Established in 1718 along the banks of the San Antonio River, the site of the mission was moved twice before finally being permanently situated in its present location. The first mission structures, a two-story tower constructed of stone and some thatched huts, or *jacales*, were destroyed by a hurricane in 1724. By 1745 sturdier buildings had been erected that included a two-story stone *convento* running north to south, offices below and living quarters above, a row of Indian huts of adobe also running north to south, and a church, west facing, that had collapsed and was under reconstruction. By 1762 the entire area had been enclosed by stone and adobe walls, forming a large rectangle. The church, still being rebuilt, was now situated outside the protecting walls to the southeast.

In 1793 religious authorities turned over control of the mission and its surrounding lands to the civilian government of San Antonio de Bexar. It was noted at the time that the church had a partially domed roof and that half of the north wall of the compound had collapsed, as had all but twelve of the twenty Indian huts along the west wall. The entire site was in various stages of abandonment and disrepair, but it was still considered a pueblo, or small town, and was referred to as Valero.

An Illustrated History of Texas Forts

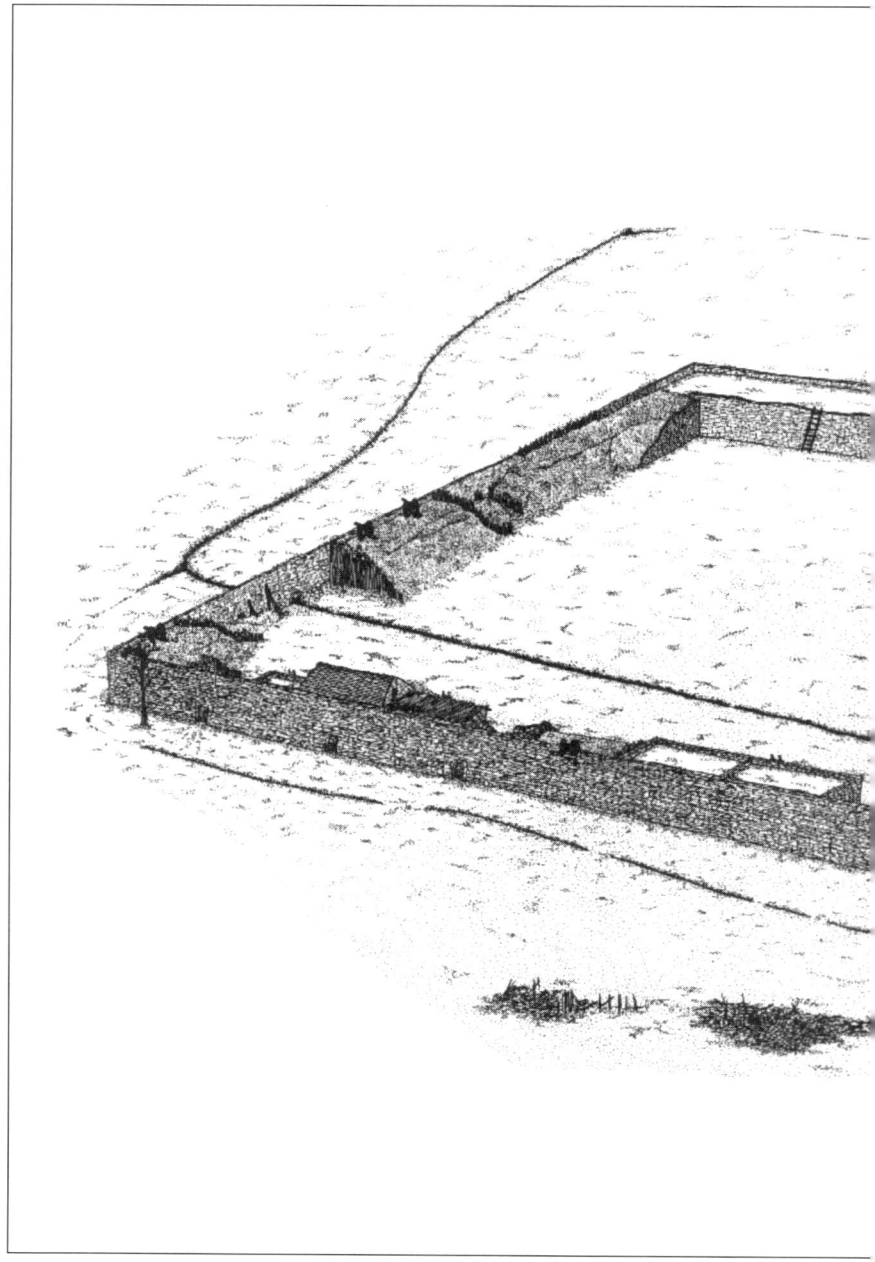

Spanish Presidio Period

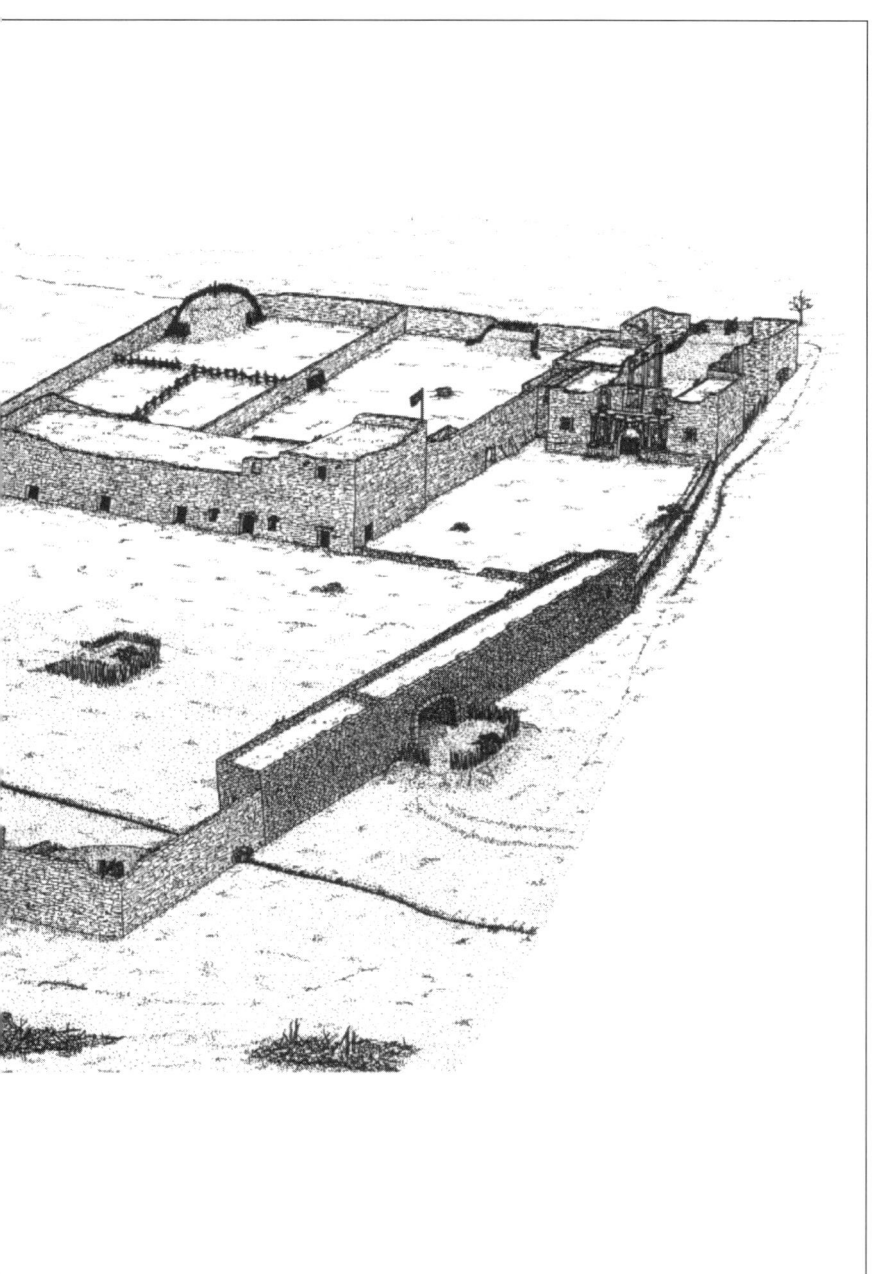

To counter the problem of illegal immigration from the United States after the Louisiana Purchase from France in 1803, the Spanish posted garrisons throughout the northern province of Tejas. The unit assigned to San Antonio was known as The Second Flying Company of San Carlos de Alamo de Parras. This 100-man company settled, with their families, south of the mission compound in the area known as La Villita, and by 1805 were using the mission buildings to house the sick. Repairs were undertaken to the structures, roofs, and walls that were completed by 1810. This was the beginning of the Alamo, a name adopted from its garrison, as a military installation and the end of San Antonio de Valero as a religious establishment.

Fortress Alamo

In the years between 1810 and 1821, rebellion ran rampant in Mexico and the Alamo was taken over several times by both sides in the conflicts. In 1810 the fort was controlled by Spanish Royalists and Mexican rebels were kept prisoner there. In 1811 the Royalists were driven out and in turn incarcerated within the walls. That same year the Royalists regained the upper hand and held the Alamo until 1813, when a rebel army, including 300 American mercenaries, overwhelmed them. But again loyal Spanish forces beat the rebels and reoccupied the fort. From 1813 to 1821 the Alamo remained firmly in the hands of the Royalists.

By 1821 Mexico had finally won independence from Spain and set up its own government. There followed many years of relative peace and quiet during which many Americans took advantage of liberal immigration policies to move into Tejas. But when Antonio Lopez de Santa Anna overthrew Mexico's president in 1832 and took control, tensions between the new

American arrivals and the Mexican government rose. While solidifying his hold on power, Santa Anna sought to stem the flow of immigration with severe restrictions. He abolished the Mexican Constitution of 1824, refused the petition from Tejas for separate statehood from Coahuila, disbanded all local governing bodies, and imposed import taxes on all foreign goods. He placed all governing authority in the hands of the military.

In October of 1835 a detachment of Mexican soldiers was sent from the Alamo to the town of Gonzales with orders to retrieve a small cannon given to the residents as a protection against Indians. Since emotions had been running high against the Mexican government for some time and colonists feared being disarmed in a time of crisis, the townspeople of Gonzales refused to give up the cannon and shots were fired. The Texas Revolution, after many previous fitful starts, now began in earnest. An army of colonists under the leadership of Stephen Austin marched on San Antonio and laid siege to the town and the Alamo.

Battles of the Alamo

Five hundred Mexican soldiers commanded by Gen. Martin Perfecto de Cos defended San Antonio and the Alamo for fifty-six days. Cos had been busy fortifying the Alamo, emplacing cannon ramps, tearing the roof off the church for material, digging trenches, and reinforcing the walls. He had ample troops to defend the fort but chose to leave only a token force there and instead dig in and defend the town. This tactic would cost him a victory when his troops were driven from San Antonio after a fierce almost five day battle in the streets, most of it at close quarters. Cos withdrew his battered forces into the Alamo, short on supplies and ammunition. Demoralized by the defeat and with no reinforcements in sight, Cos surrendered in December. He and his remaining men were allowed to march south for home under their promise not to take up arms against Tejas again. At that same moment, Gen. Santa Anna, president of Mexico, was marching north at the head of a vast army, intent on crushing the rebellion.

By February of 1836 command of the garrison at San Antonio was jointly held by Col. William B. Travis and Col. James Bowie. Both men believed that holding the Alamo was key to the success of the revolution. Chief engineer Green B. Jameson worked tirelessly shoring up defenses, mounting cannon captured from Cos, and planning future improvements to the fort. While most of the men from the attacking forces of the previous December had either gone home or joined an ill-fated expedition against the Mexican town of Matamoros, morale was kept high among the remaining men by the arrival of famed frontiersman David Crockett from Tennessee. But belief in the cause was not enough to overcome the fact that there were less than 200 men to defend the Alamo, an area of almost three acres that required at least 500 men to defend adequately. On February 23 leading elements of the Mexican army marched into San Antonio, Santa Anna at their head, unopposed. The Texians had already withdrawn inside the Alamo.

As more and more units of the Mexican army arrived and encircled the Alamo, artillery began to bombard the fort continuously day and night. Mexican infantry probed the defenses, searching for weaknesses, and the massed regimental bands played music nightly. All this activity was designed to wear the defenders down, deprive them of rest, and cause them to use up their supply of powder and shot. Travis, in sole command due to the sudden illness of Bowie, bided his time

Spanish Presidio Period

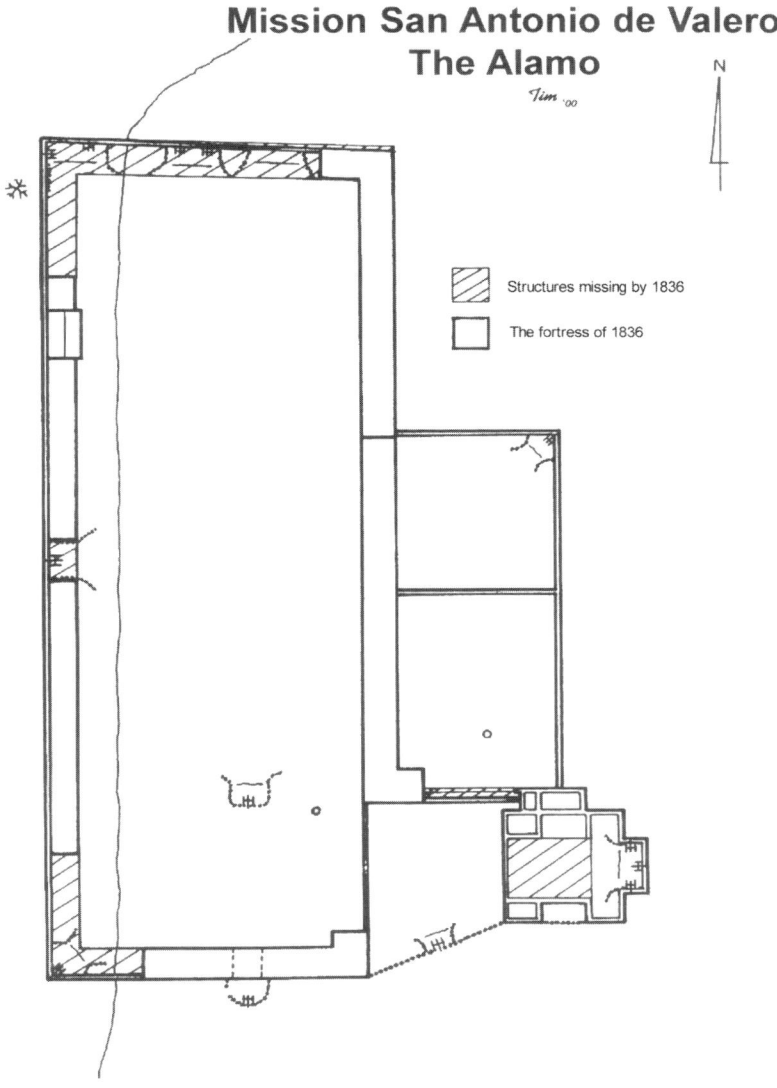

and sent out messengers seeking reinforcements and supplies. Some men did heed Travis's appeals and made their way through the Mexican lines into the Alamo. But when large numbers of men failed to rush to the rescue, the outcome of the siege was a certainty. The defenders, however, chose to remain in the Alamo.

At 5:00 A.M. on the morning of March 6, 1836, Mexican infantrymen charged out of the predawn darkness and raced toward the fort from all sides. The order of attack issued by Gen. Santa Anna had been precise down to the last detail, but within minutes the rifle and cannon fire from the awakened defenders had reduced the assault force to a howling, clawing mob. Twice the Mexicans were thrown back with terrible losses, twice they were reorganized and surged forward again. Santa Anna committed his reserves on the third assault, and his battered, bloody troops managed to gain the top of the north wall.

The stout old walls of the Alamo had stood like a dam against three crashing waves of Mexican soldiers. Now the

Spanish Presidio Period

dam had crumbled and the defenders were swept away by the tide of attackers. As the Mexicans poured over the walls, the battle became nothing more than a deadly, bloody brawl in the dark. Building by building, room by room, the fighting raged within the compound. By dawn the Alamo had been taken, the defenders killed, and a third of the attacking force dead or dying. Only 90 minutes had elapsed from start to finish. The few prisoners taken were executed, the women, children, and a few slaves were freed, and the bodies of the Alamo garrison were piled up and burned outside the walls.

As Santa Anna's army continued to advance into the interior of Tejas, the Alamo was repaired and improved. Situated now on the Mexican line of supply and communication, it would serve as a depot and bastion against attack. But by May, after Santa Anna's defeat and capture in April by Sam Houston, the fortifications were ordered destroyed as the Mexican army retreated from the Republic of Texas. The walls were torn down, the cannons were disabled, and everything flammable was burned. The Alamo was abandoned. Eventually, local townspeople picked through the rubble and carried away tons of stones to construct new housing as the town of San Antonio grew and expanded.

Later History

In the late 1840s the U.S. Army took over what remained of the Alamo—the church, the long barrack (formerly known as the *convento*), a small portion of the south wall, and several small buildings that once stood inside the north and west walls—for use as a supply depot. The long barrack and church were roofed, the distinctive hump on the church facade was added in 1850, and large amounts of supplies and ammunition were stored at the site. All the while, construction of new homes and streets had begun all around, and even within, the old compound. The town of San Antonio was slowly engulfing the Alamo.

In February of 1861, two months before the bombardment of Fort Sumter in South Carolina would start the Civil War, a group of Texas secessionists seized the Alamo and the supplies stored there. This action was supported by the U.S. Army commander of the installation and was a bloodless affair. During the Civil War the Alamo was used as it had been previously, as a supply depot for the Confederate army in Texas. After the war, the victorious U.S. Army reoccupied the site until 1876, when Fort Sam Houston was constructed nearby and the troops were transferred there. By 1877 Honore Grenet had purchased the site and turned the long barrack into a grocery store, adding a wooden facade, second story porches, and wooden towers to the building. The church remained untouched.

In 1884 the partnership of Hugo & Schmeltzer bought out Grenet and continued to operate the mercantile business. At this time the only structures remaining were the church, now

owned by the state of Texas, and the remodeled long barrack. The small portion of the south wall and the remaining buildings of the north and west walls had long since been demolished. Paved streets and electric light poles crisscrossed the area around the remains of the Alamo, and the city pressed in on all sides. In 1905, with financial aid from the state and using their own funds, a group known as the Daughters of the Republic of Texas (DRT) purchased the long barrack building.

An Illustrated History of Texas Forts

The state of Texas turned over control of the church to the group, which began to plan renovations to both structures and to purchase all available property around the area.

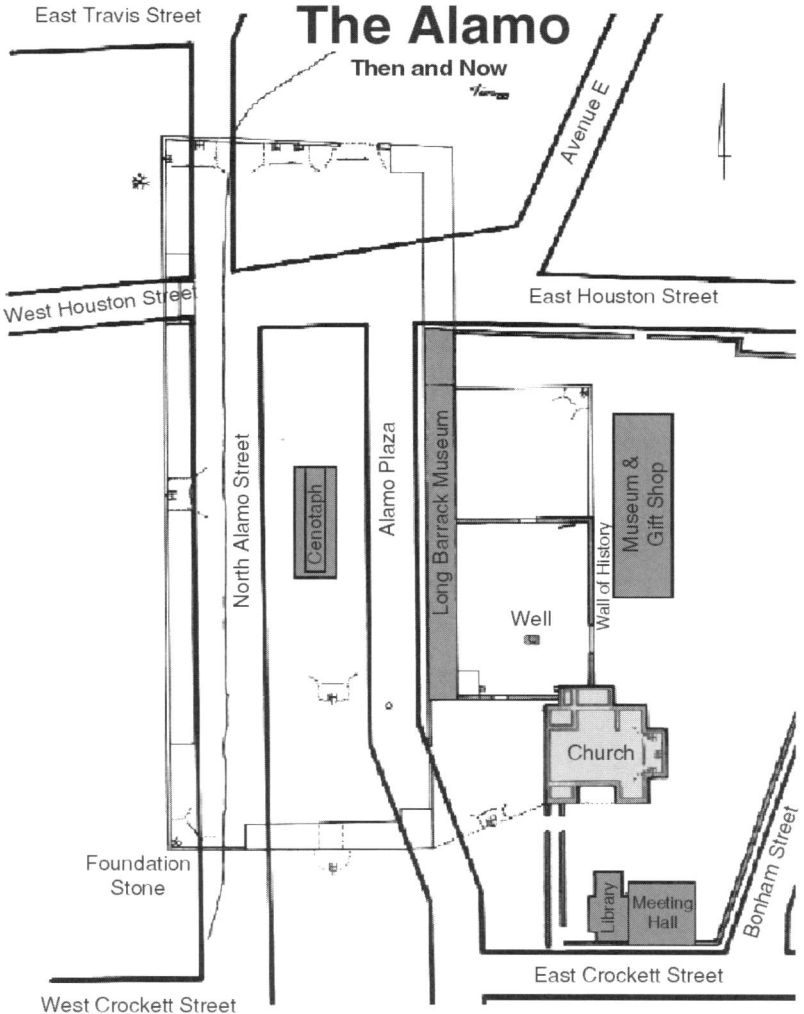

Spanish Presidio Period

Between 1912 and 1918 all wooden additions attached to the long barrack were removed and the remains of the second story of the building was torn off. This made the church the visual center of attention as the tallest structure. Land acquired to the east of the long barrack and church was enclosed with a wall to create a park-like setting of four acres. The long barrack became a museum and the church a shrine to the memory of the fallen defenders of 1836. A museum and gift shop was built in 1936, east of the long barrack and north of the church, and in 1939 a cenotaph, or empty tomb, monument by famed Italian sculptor Pompeo Coppini was erected at the site of the former Alamo Plaza. A research library was added south of the church in 1950. A visual Wall of History was put in place in 1997 adjacent to the museum/gift store, and plans are now underway to place visual historic markers around the area showing artistic renderings of the original compound from each location. Approximately three million people from around the world visit the Alamo every year.

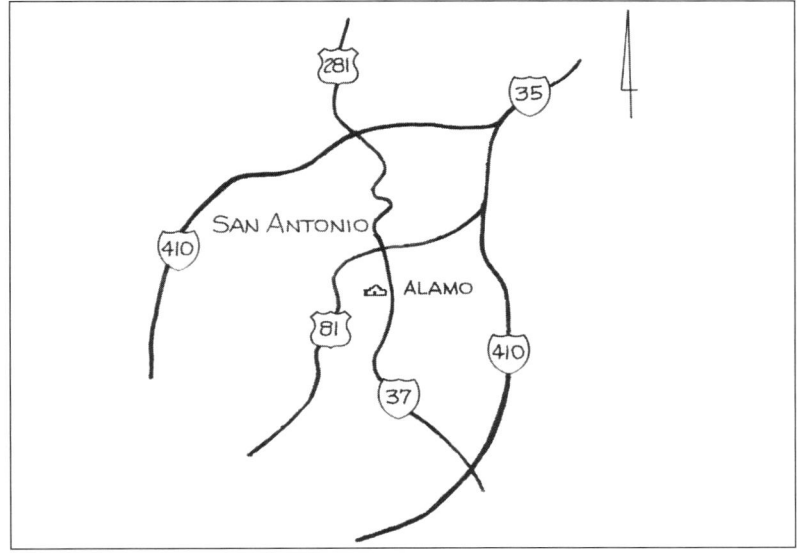

The Alamo, located on North Alamo Street between East Houston and East Crockett Streets, is open Monday-Saturday, 9:00 A.M. to 5:30 P.M. and Sunday, 10:00 A.M. to 5:30 P.M. Admission is free but donations are welcome.

There is some question regarding whether or not the Presidio San Antonio de Bexar was ever actually constructed. Two maps exist, from 1722 and 1730, that show a distinctive square enclosure with cannon bastions at each corner. Two other maps, from 1764 and 1776, do not show any such enclosure, but do call the same map area the presidio.

Presidio San Antonio de Bexar

In 1718 the first presidio was located on the west side of the San Antonio River approximately a quarter of a mile from the Mission San Antonio de Valero. It was relocated in 1722 to a site directly across the river from the mission. It is probable that at that time some form of stockade walls were erected and adobe houses were built inside. By 1726 the garrison numbered over fifty men, and the population of the town growing up around the presidio was close to two hundred.

Within fifty years the town of San Antonio was the official capital of the province of Tejas. The presidio walls had disappeared by now, but a hollow square of houses marked the location, and the open area inside was known as Military Plaza. In 1772 the commander of the presidio was designated as the governor of Tejas, thus holding both military and civilian authority. Within twenty years the Mission San Antonio de Valero would begin to serve more as a military installation

Spanish Presidio Period

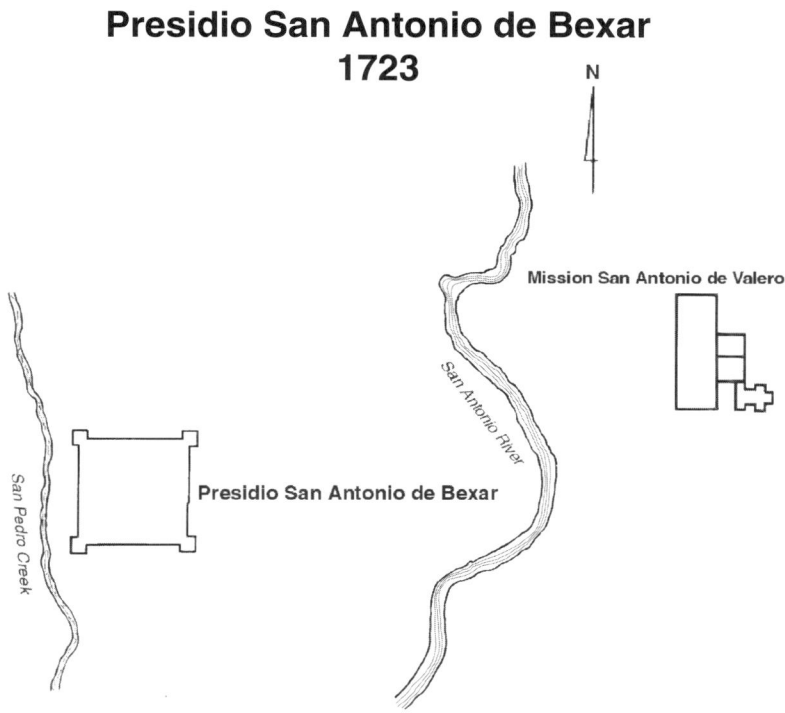

and the Presidio San Antonio would cease to exist. By 1803 the mission was known as the Alamo and became the fort across the river. Military Plaza and Plaza de la Constitucion, separated by San Fernando Church, became the principle defensive positions within the town.

During the siege of San Antonio in 1835, at the beginning of the Texas Revolution, Mexican commander Gen. Martin Perfecto de Cos defended the town from strong positions around Military Plaza. On December 5 the Texian army assaulted the town and, after two days of savage house-to-house fighting, ousted the Mexican soldiers from San Antonio. After Gen. Antonio Lopez de Santa Anna reoccupied the town in 1836 and overran the Alamo, the site of the presidio would never again serve in any real military capacity.

Later History

Today the Spanish Governor's Palace, former home of the presidio commander situated on the west side of the compound, still stands on Camaron Street in San Antonio. It is an often visited tourist attraction and is open Monday through Saturday from 9 A.M. to 5 P.M. and Sunday from 10 A.M. to 5 P.M. Admission is charged. The Military Plaza area is now bounded by Commerce, Laredo, Dolorosa, and Flores Streets.

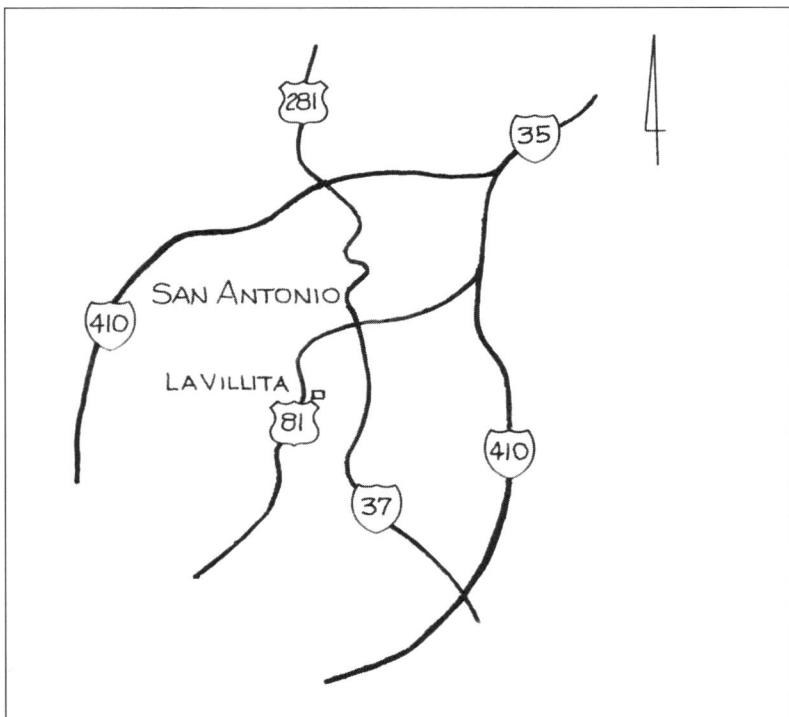

The Presidio Nuestra Señora de Loreto came to be known by many names during its existence. It was called Nuestra Señora Santa Maria de Loreto de la Bahia del Espiritu Santo, more popularly La Bahia, Fort Goliad, and finally Fort Defiance. In 1836 more revolutionary soldiers would die there than in all the battles of the Texas Revolution combined.

Presidio Nuestra Señora de Loreto

In 1721 the presidio was established on the ruins of LaSalle's ill-fated Fort St. Louis in reaction to a perceived threat of encroachment on Spanish territory by the French. The presidio also served as protection for the Mission Nuestra Señora del Espiritu Santo de Zuniga. Located on the banks of Garcitas Creek near Matagorda and Lavaca Bays, it was octagonal in shape, had four bastions, a tower, and was surrounded by a moat. By early 1723 the garrison numbered nearly one hundred men, and the presidio was considered one of the most efficiently operated outposts in the province. But since the nearby mission was failing in its efforts with the local Karankawa Indians, Spanish authorities decided to relocate both establishments about twenty-six miles inland and try their luck with the Aranama Indians. The move took place in 1726, and the nickname of La Bahia, The Bay, accompanied the presidio to its new location.

Presidio La Bahia

For the next twenty-six years La Bahia was to prosper at its site on the Guadalupe River. Both the presidio and nearby mission were models of self-sustaining outposts, with successful farming and cattle ranching enabling them to feed not only themselves but other Tejas missions as well. With the possible exception of a few difficulties with the Karankawa at its previous location, the presidio garrison did not mount any major military operations against any hostile forces in either an offensive or defensive posture. It was a peaceful, productive life.

That would change in 1749, however, when the presidio and mission were moved again another twenty-six miles inland. Under a reorganization plan from Spain to consolidate military outposts in Tejas, La Bahia was established on the banks of the San Antonio River and assumed the duty of guarding El Camino Real, The King's Highway. The Mission Espiritu Santo was incorporated with the existing Nuestra Señora del Rosario Mission and Mission Nuestra Señora del Refugio in 1793, under the guardianship of the presidio. All were eventually grouped together under the name of La Bahia, as was the village that grew up nearby.

Troops from the garrison provided escort for convoys and supply trains on El Camino Real and repelled Lipan Apache and Comanche attacks in the area of the missions and the town throughout the 1750s. Once again, as before, the area around the presidio prospered. The fort itself contained a large barracks building, forty houses for the married men of the garrison and their families, a church where all could attend services without having to travel to a nearby mission, and was armed with six cannon. In the late 1760s Presidio La Bahia was one of only two military outposts not ordered abandoned by royal decree; San Antonio de Bexar was the other. La Bahia became the only Spanish presidio in the Gulf Coast area of Tejas, even though it was over fifty miles from the sea.

The nineteenth century brought a prolonged period of conflict and strife to Mexico in which Presidio La Bahia played

Spanish Presidio Period

an ongoing role. In 1812 the Magee-Gutierrez filibusters captured the presidio during their attempt to declare Tejas independent from Mexico. The ragtag army of Mexican, American, and Indian invaders were bottled up in La Bahia by Spanish troops in a siege that lasted almost four months. When the Spanish lifted the siege and left, the rebels moved on to San Antonio de Bexar and ultimate defeat. In 1817 a group of American veterans of the War of 1812 led by Col. Henry Perry tried to capture La Bahia but were repulsed with heavy losses.

The year 1821 saw the return of Dr. James Long, leader of a failed revolution in 1819 that flourished and died in Nacogdoches. Landing at Matagoda Bay, Long led his filibusters inland and captured La Bahia without a fight. The garrison from San Antonio, some ninety miles away, quickly rushed to the scene and after a two day battle took Long and his followers prisoner, sending them to disappear into prison in Mexico City. Later that year Mexico's revolution against Spain was successful and the presidio was regarrisoned by Mexican soldiers.

Fort Goliad

During the period of American immigration in the 1820s, Presidio La Bahia became the protector of DeWitt's colony, DeLeon's colony, and the Power/Hewetson colony. In 1829

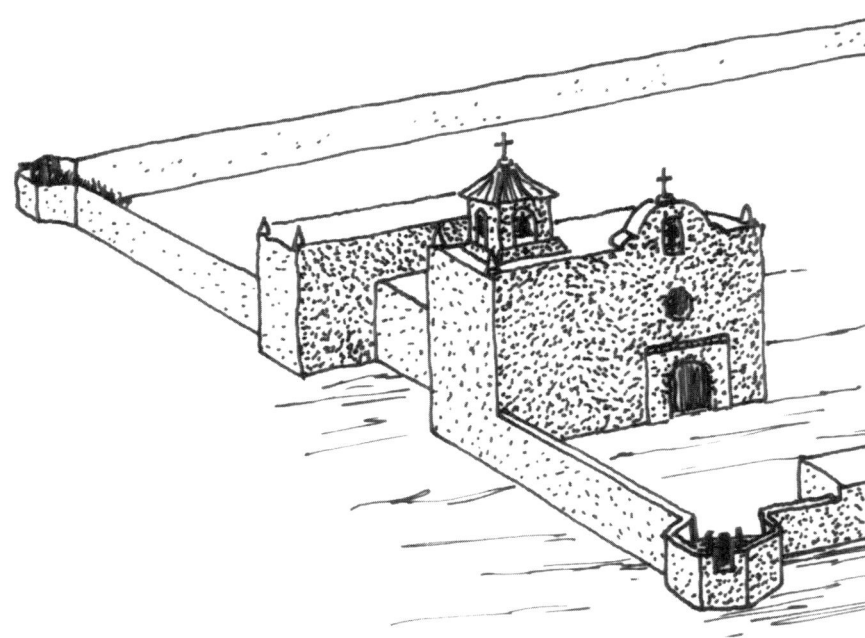

the name of the town that had been born and flourished near the presidio walls was officially changed from La Bahia to Goliad. The presidio retained its familiar name.

With the outbreak of the Texas Revolution in 1835, Presidio La Bahia became a post of military significance. Situated near three major roadways—The King's Highway from Mexico City to Nacogdoches, The Atacosito Road (La Bahia Road) from Goliad to Washington-on-the-Brazos, and the road from the port of El Copano to San Antonio—La Bahia was in a perfect position to harry, or support, movements of troops and supplies on those routes. The colonists in revolt were not slow to recognize that fact, and George Collinsworth led an armed group to Goliad intending to capture the strategic presidio. Before dawn on October 10, the Texians rushed into the compound and took the post commander, Lt. Col. Francisco Sandoval, prisoner in his quarters. Shots were exchanged

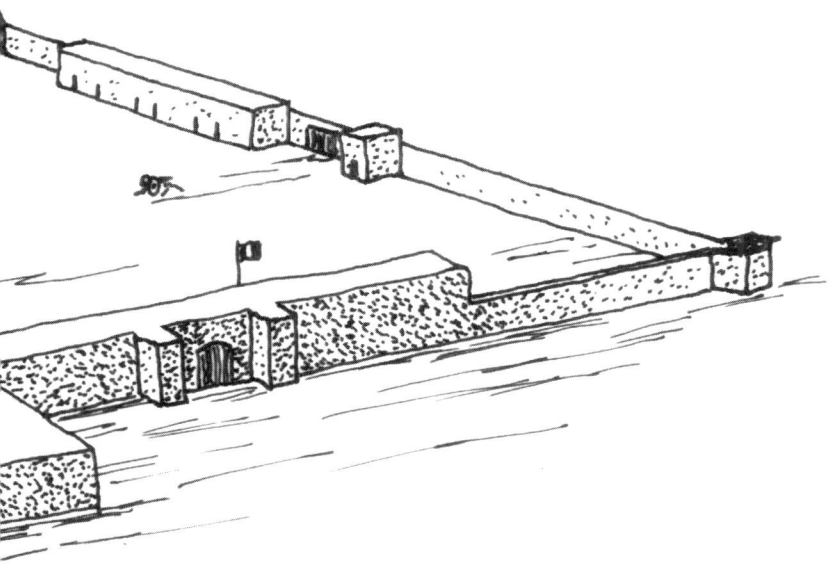

with the awakening Mexican soldiers in their barracks. A freed black man, Sam McCulloch, was the only attacker wounded during the firefight, and within thirty minutes the garrison surrendered.

Now the revolution had shifted to San Antonio and Philip Dimitt assumed command at La Bahia, renaming it Fort Goliad. In San Antonio, Gen. Martin Perfecto de Cos was besieged by the Texian army and cut off from any resupply from El Copano by Fort Goliad's position on the only road to the sea. Dimitt sent out punitive expeditions against areas he suspected to be staging sites for a Mexican army attempt to recapture Goliad. Small actions were fought at Fort Lipantitlan near San Patricio and at the Nueces River that saw the Texian forces victorious and the Mexicans left disorganized. For the moment, Goliad was safe from any organized counterattack, but when Gen. Cos surrendered San Antonio in December of 1835, events were set in motion that would write a terrible, bloody chapter in the history of Texas and of Goliad.

Fort Defiance

In early February of 1836, Col. James W. Fannin was at Goliad to oversee and organize the arrival of hundreds of volunteers from the United States who came to join the revolution. Fannin was a brave and able subordinate officer, having served with distinction under the command of Col. James Bowie at the battle of Concepcion during the siege of San Antonio, but he lacked the self-confidence and decisiveness to command on his own. Following the defeat of Gen. Cos at San Antonio, a period of political chaos engulfed the provisional government of Texas. Nobody seemed to know who was in charge at any given time in any given capacity.

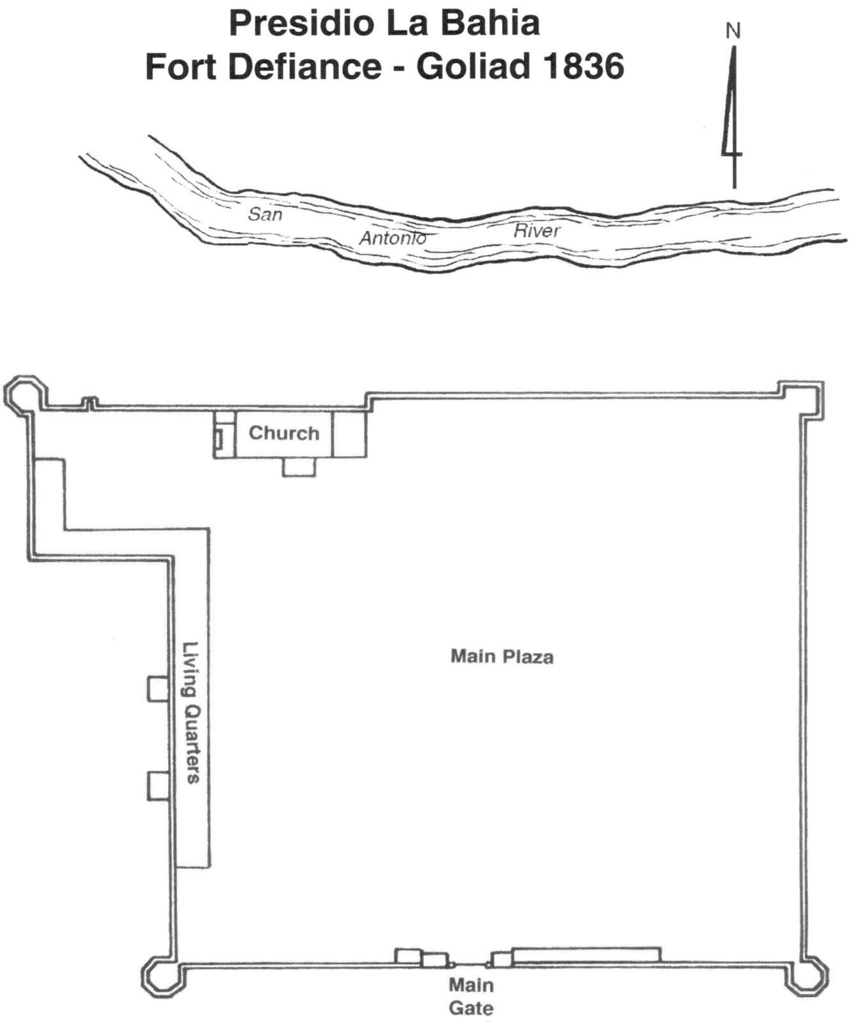

Spanish Presidio Period

After a map drawn by Joseph M. Chadwick in 1836

Orders were issued and withdrawn, plans were made and then discarded. Somehow, perhaps in view of the fact he had spent two years at West Point, Fannin emerged with sole command of the garrison at Goliad. He set about repairing and improving the defenses of the fort, renaming it Fort Defiance.

There were 420 men in the garrison at Goliad, 150 men at the Alamo in San Antonio. But, throughout the Mexican siege of the Alamo from February 23 to March 6, Fannin refused to budge from Fort Defiance to answer repeated calls for reinforcements and supplies from that doomed fortress. He did make a half-hearted attempt to march his men to San Antonio on February 28 but returned to Goliad after a wagon broke down less than a mile into the journey. After the Alamo fell, Fannin received orders from the commander of the Texas army, Gen. Sam Houston, to abandon Goliad and fall back to the town of Gonzales, where the army was consolidating its forces. Fannin wasted more than a week getting started, for a variety of reasons good and bad. Lead elements of the Mexican force coming to attack Fort Defiance were already in sight when the garrison finally began to withdraw on the morning of March 19.

That afternoon the unmounted men were overtaken by Mexican cavalry on the open prairie near Coleto Creek. From a defensive square made up of their wagons and baggage, the Texians fought off repeated infantry and cavalry attacks until night fell and hostilities ceased. The next day Fannin, himself wounded in the previous day's fighting, surrendered to the Mexican commander, Gen. Jose Cosme Urrea, and his men were then marched back to Goliad to be held prisoner in the same fort they had vacated just the day before.

Spanish Presidio Period

On Palm Sunday, March 27, the prisoners were separated into three groups and marched out of the fort under heavy guard. Those too sick or wounded, including Fannin, to join their comrades were left behind at Fort Defiance. Each group of captives was marched away in a different direction. Just outside of Goliad, but still within hearing distance of the town, the Mexicans halted each group and opened fire on the unarmed men. Survivors of the first volley, wounded or unharmed, were finished off with bayonets, cavalry lances, swords, and pistols. The wounded and sick prisoners back at Fort Defiance were executed by their guards.

Three hundred forty-two prisoners were massacred; only twenty-eight managed to run for their lives and escape the carnage.

Later History

After the Texas Revolution the presidio at Goliad fell into disrepair. It was occupied briefly by Mexican troops that invaded the Republic of Texas in 1842 but generally was never used as a fort again. In fact, between 1846 and 1853 the presidio church was used as a private residence by Judge Pryor Lea, who grew vegetables in the old main plaza parade grounds. In 1853 the Catholic Church established its ownership of the site and began to conduct services in the church, the only building still in reasonably good condition.

The church was restored as a New Deal public works project in 1935, as was the nearby Mission Espiritu Santo. Between 1963 and 1967 the Kathryn Stoner O'Connor foundation funded a complete restoration and reconstruction of the entire presidio complex. The site was dedicated as both a state and federal historic landmark in the late 1960s.

Spanish Presidio Period

Today the restored Presidio La Bahia is considered to be the finest example of a complete Spanish presidio in the United States. In the museum are artifacts discovered during the reconstruction and displays of items of the entire history of La Bahia with special emphasis on the Texas Revolution. Located two miles south off U.S. route 183 in Goliad, the Presidio La Bahia is open daily 9 A.M. to 4:45 P.M. except major holidays. Admission of $3.00 for adults and $1.00 for children is charged. Religious services are still regularly held in the church.

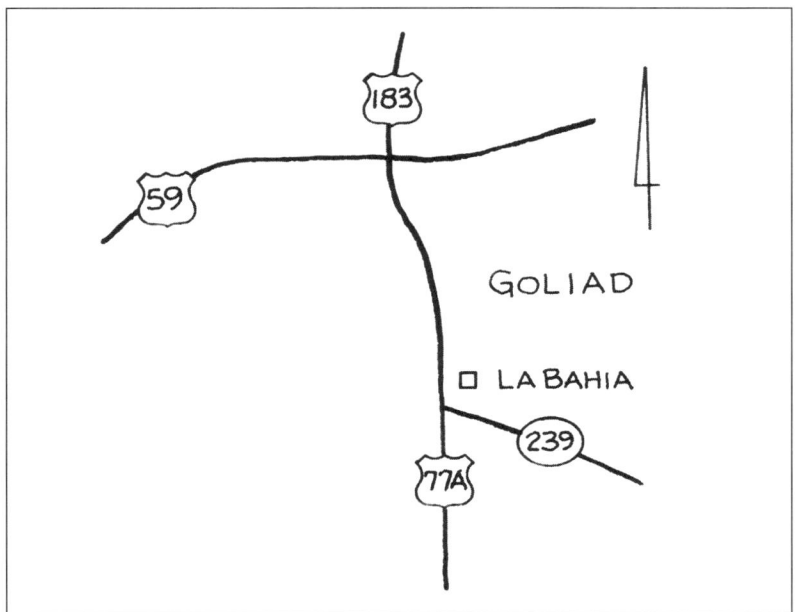

Fuerte de Santa Cruz del Cibolo

Established in 1734 at a natural ford on Cibolo Creek known as Carvajal Crossing, the fort was halfway between Presidio San Antonio de Bexar and Presidio La Bahia. This fort was not located to protect a local mission but many nearby ranches in the area from Apache raids. The garrison was made up of troops from San Antonio who had been reinforced with soldiers from Presidio Los Adaes and Presidio La Bahia. In addition to scouting for raiding Apaches, the soldiers also guarded the Presidio San Antonio horse herd sheltered in Arroyo del Cibolo.

Twice in 1737 the Apaches staged devastating raids on the herd, forcing officials in San Antonio to reconsider the wisdom of quartering the horses so far away, over twenty miles, from the town. It was decided that the horse herd would be brought back, along with the garrison of the fort. El Cibolo was abandoned, and the local ranchers were left to fend for themselves.

In 1771 the small fort was regarrisoned as part of a realignment of the presidio system in Tejas. The sturdy stockade still stood, and the interior houses were in relatively good condition. The ranchers nearby flocked to the fort to build their own quarters in and around the site if future Indian attacks forced them to take shelter there. When monthly mail service was instituted in 1779, soldiers from the fort delivered letters between San Antonio and La Bahia.

In 1782 Fuerte de Santa Cruz del Cibolo was ordered abandoned and destroyed. The area was more settled and the Indian threat had moved elsewhere so the troops were reassigned to other garrisons on the frontier.

The site of the fort, now on private property, bears no remains of the installation today.

The Presidio de Nuestra Señora de las Caldas de Guajoquilla was established in 1752. It was moved north twice along the Rio Grande before reaching its final location on the west side of the river near the site of present-day El Paso. It was renamed San Elizario in 1789.

Presidio San Elizario

As American explorers and traders increasingly "dropped in" on Santa Fe (New Mexico) to check on trade prospects in the early 1800s, San Elizario served as a detention point for many unwelcome visitors to Spanish territory.

In 1807 Zebulon Pike, of the U.S. Army, was arrested in Santa Fe and shipped south, under guard, to be incarcerated at San Elizario. His covert incursion, of which he wrote about after his eventual release, led to an influx of American traders bearing goods to offer in the closed Spanish market. All were arrested, their merchandise confiscated, and they were confined in the presidio. At the end of the Mexican Revolution in 1821, the new government began to cut back on funding and supplies for many far-flung presidios. In 1831 the ration program for San Elizario was terminated, and living conditions in the arid climate of extreme west Tejas deteriorated rapidly.

Additionally, the Rio Grande cut new channels nearby that effectively placed the presidio on an island. By 1846 the presidio was abandoned and in ruins. Rechanneling of the Rio Grande once again moved the location of the presidio without moving the actual facility itself. In 1851 most of the material used to erect the walls and buildings was carted away by local people for use in constructing their own residences.

The soldiers' chapel of Presidio San Elizario, built in 1777, survived and was maintained. Services are still held there to this day in the city of El Paso.

The area and town of Nacogdoches was the gateway to eastern Tejas from French Louisiana and the southern United States. At first envisioned as a trading depot, it was later considered by the Spanish and Mexicans as a bulwark against incursions from the east by the French and Americans. But it would never hold back any invasion, becoming instead the headquarters for just about every rebellion brought to Tejas by outside and internal forces.

The Y'Barbo House

In 1716 the Spanish mission of Nuestra Señora de Guadalupe de los Nacogdoches was founded in eastern Tejas among the Nacogdoche Indians. Situated on El Camino Real, or The King's Highway, a trail blazed in 1691 that connected Mexico City with its northern province and French Louisiana, the mission never succeeded and was abandoned in 1773. Many of the mission buildings became the first homes of the town of Nacogdoches.

By 1779 Don Antonio Gil Y'Barbo had erected a home for himself in the town, utilizing primarily stone in constructing the two-story building. The influence of French colonial architecture was clearly evident in the structure, no doubt influenced by Y'Barbo's frequent contact with the French traders in Louisiana, and it would eventually be used for a variety of activities because of its solid construction. The home would serve as a trading post, a public building, and a fort over the years to come.

The Stone Fort

In 1812 Nacogdoches fell to an invading force out of Louisiana. Attempting to separate Tejas from Mexico and declare it an independent entity, the invaders, called "filibusters," under the joint leadership of Bernardo Gutierrez de Lara and Augustus Magee, moved easily across Tejas as far as San Antonio de Bexar. The Magee-Gutierrez expedition, as it was known, scored several military victories before being finally defeated and destroyed by Spanish forces at the battle of Medina. The Stone Fort at Nacogdoches, the first headquarters of the doomed expedition, would thereafter serve as a command post for every revolution to follow.

In 1819 Dr. James Long marched into Nacogdoches at the head of another force of invaders, with the same intention of wresting Tejas from Spanish control as did Magee and Gutierrez. But Long would not enjoy any of the successes of the previous invaders. Establishing the seat of his new republic at the Stone Fort, he set off for Galveston Island, to the

south, in an attempt to enlist the aid of the infamous pirate Jean Lafitte. While Lafitte was refusing to help prop up Long's fledgling government, a Spanish force fell on Nacogdoches and decisively defeated the invaders. Long returned to a deserted town, his forces and sympathizers beaten and fled. He returned to the United States in defeat.

As the Spanish had resisted revolutions out of Nacogdoches, so too did the Mexican government have to field troops against that stronghold. In 1826 empresario Haden Edwards, unhappy with Mexican handling of land grants for his colony and disputes over property ownership with older residents, declared his area, Nacogdoches, the independent Republic of Fredonia. Once again the Stone Fort saw service as a headquarters and fort for yet another revolutionary movement. Also once again, government troops, this time Mexican, drove the disorganized rebels from their position of strength and ended the rebellion. There followed a few years of relative calm while the seeds of the Texas Revolution grew and began to bear fruit.

In 1832 armed conflict erupted when the Mexican garrison commander of Nacogdoches, Col. Jose de las Piedras, attempted to enforce an order from Mexico City to disarm the local American colonists. The angry colonists advanced on Nacogdoches prepared for an armed confrontation, and Piedras, unable to concentrate his troops at the unfinished Fort Teran nearby (see the Texas Revolution section) instead occupied and fortified several houses in town including the Stone Fort.

Mexican cavalry turned back one group of colonists outside of town, but another group managed to enter and fought the soldiers from house to house. When the cavalry was outflanked and forced to retreat, Piedras abandoned Nacogdoches and withdrew along the Angelina River. After a running fight of several miles, the Mexicans surrendered to the colonists and were eventually sent home to Mexico on parole.

During the Texas Revolution of 1835-36, Nacogdoches served as a conduit for idealistic volunteers from the United States who came to join the army of independence. The Stone Fort once again became a headquarters. Within sight of the structure, or even within its walls, the oath of allegiance to the Republic of Texas was administered to hundreds of recently arrived volunteers, including the famous David Crockett of Tennessee. From Nacogdoches the newly enlisted soldiers of the revolution were sent to the Texas frontier to confront the Mexican army. Many, including Crockett, would later die defending the Alamo in far-off San Antonio de Bexar. This time the venerable old Stone Fort, having been the site of much previous bloodshed during earlier invasions and rebellions, would be spared the ravages of combat in this successful war for liberation.

Later History

My the mid-1800s, the Stone Fort was popularly known as the "Old Stone Fort Saloon," having been converted to that purpose by its owner. After passing through the hands of many other owners and serving a variety of uses as the years passed, the Stone Fort was purchased in 1901 and scheduled for demolition to make way for a more modern structure. A local historical society, the Cum Concillio Club, bought the stones of the building after it was taken down.

In 1936 using early photographs of the building as a guide, the Stone Fort was reconstructed with its original stones on the campus of Stephen F. Austin State University in Nacogdoches. Today it is a museum, its collection of artifacts devoted primarily to the period of local history from the first Spanish settlement to the Texas Revolution. Located off North Street, Highway 59, in Nacgdoches at the intersection of campus roads College Drive and Griffith Boulevard, the Stone Fort Museum is open Tuesday through Saturday 9 A.M. to 5 P.M. and Sunday 1 P.M. to 5 P.M.

Admission is free (museum operations are funded by gift shop sales revenues), and guided tours are available by reservation only by calling (409) 568-2408.

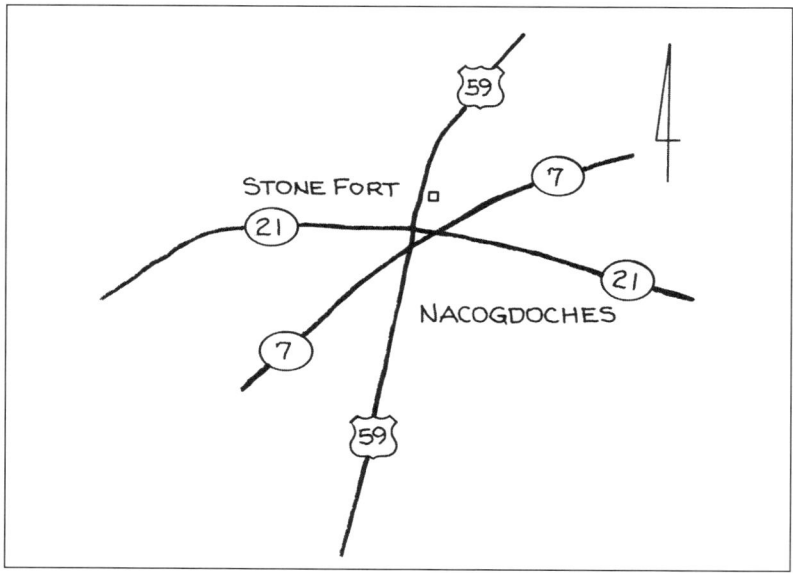

East Tejas Presidios

In 1721 the Marques de Aguayo established two presidios in the extreme eastern area of the province.

Presidio Nuestra Señora de los Dolores de los Tejas had been built in 1716 on the east bank of the Neches River and abandoned in 1719 after a French invasion of east Tejas. The Marques rebuilt the presidio four miles from the Angelina River (near present-day Douglass). Presidio Nuestra Señora del Pilar de los Adaes was constructed as the furthermost outpost of the province to check any further French expansion.

Presidio de los Tejas was abandoned in 1729 because the peaceful attitude of the local Indians made a military presence unnecessary. Presidio de los Adaes was abandoned in 1763 after Spain acquired the Louisiana Territory from France in a secret treaty.

The site of Presidio Nuestra Señora de los Dolores de los Tejas is marked by a state historical marker on FM 225, six miles south of Douglass.

The site of Presidio Nuestra Señora del Pilar de los Adaes can be found near Natchitoches, Louisiana, in the Los Adaes State Commemorative Area, 10 miles west off SR 6.

In 1751 the Presidio San Francisco Xavier de Gigedo was established on the south bank of the San Gabriel River, known then as the San Xavier River. The presidio suffered bad fortune from the very beginning.

The governor of Tejas, Pedro Espriella, was opposed to the establishment of the presidio, and when the authorities in Mexico City ignored his wishes, he refused to assign a proper number of soldiers to garrison the facility. Relations between the military and the San Xavier missionaries were venomous. The presidio commander was implicated in the murder of a

Presidio de los Adaes
1763

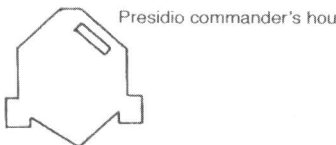

Presidio Nuestra Senora del Pilar de los Adaes

Mission San Miguel de Linares de los Adaes

Presidio commander's house

Spanish Presidio Period

local missionary and a Spanish soldier shortly after assuming command and was removed from his position. By 1755, only four years after its beginning, the presidio had been through scandal, disease, drought, and official neglect.

The presidio commander at the time simply gave up and moved his men to the San Marcos River without orders to do so in 1755. Presidio de Gigedo was never reoccupied, and its former garrison was reassigned to the Presidio San Luis de las Amarillas on the San Saba River in 1757.

The presidio was located about five miles from the present-day town of Rockdale, in Milam County.

When Presidio San Agustin de Ahumada was established on the east bank of the Trinity River in 1756, a series of incidents would begin that would rival a modern day soap opera. Situated on the site of a former French trading post, the presidio and the mission, Nuestra Señora de la Luz, suffered from disease and lack of supplies from the onset. In 1759, to avert open warfare with the local Orcoquiza Indians, a Spanish soldier was publically executed for murdering a tribesman. The lieutenant in charge of the presidio, after ordering the execution, then petitioned the government for the assignment of a captain to command the garrison.

In 1763 a captain was sent, but his methods of command were so harsh that eighteen soldiers promptly deserted. Taking refuge with the French to the east, the soldiers pled their case to the Spanish authorities, and the governor agreed to replace the presidio commander. Another lieutenant and a detachment of twenty soldiers arrived in 1764 with orders to arrest the captain. The presidio commander refused to submit to arrest and barricaded himself in his house. To smoke him out, the house was set on fire.

The resulting blaze destroyed the captain's house, the governor's home, and several soldiers' barracks. In the confusion the captain escaped. He would later clear his name and assume command again in 1769. The lieutenant who had commanded the presidio before, who had requested the captain's assignment, was arrested in 1765 and charged with perjury and for his part in helping start the devastating fire. To add insult to injury, in 1766 a hurricane blew in from the Gulf and leveled what remained of the presidio and the nearby mission. The presidio was rebuilt a short distance to the east of its original location.

By 1772 the outpost was officially declared obsolete and its abandonment was ordered. At that time only three soldiers and one missionary manned the site and were delighted to leave. The majority of the garrison had already been reassigned, in 1771, to combat the Apache far to the west.

No trace of Presidio San Agustin de Ahumada remains today, but speculation and some archeological study would place its location forty miles west of present-day Beaumont near the town of Wallisville.

The San Luis de las Amarillas Presidio and the Mission Santa Cruz de San Saba that it was to protect were isolated outposts amid a sea of hostile Indian tribes. Long after the mission was destroyed and the presidio was abandoned, the area they occupied became famous in Texas history for a heroic event involving the legendary James Bowie.

Presidio San Luis de las Amarillas

The presidio was established on the north bank of the San Saba River in 1757. Spanish authorities had determined that the best way to curb Indian raids on San Antonio that originated in the San Saba area was to bring a mission and religion to the Lipan Apaches there. Conflicts between the presidio commander and the mission priests caused the fathers to construct their mission on the south side of the San Saba River four miles from the presidio. This move to avoid friction with the military suited the local Comanche just fine.

In perhaps the first major collision between the Spanish and Comanche, 2,000 warriors swept down on Mission de

San Saba in March of 1758. Eight mission occupants were killed outright, including two of the three mission priests, and the survivors barricaded themselves in the buildings while the compound was looted and set on fire by the raiders. At the presidio, work details and other assignments had reduced the garrison from 100 men to less than a third of that number. No rescue force could be sent to the mission. After dark, a small detachment of soldiers was sent to the mission to ascertain the situation. Discovering twenty-seven survivors at the burning mission, the soldiers escorted them safely back to the presidio.

The presidio was surrounded the next day but was not attacked. A day or so later the horde of warriors simply withdrew from the area. The mission was never rebuilt.

Real Presidio de San Saba

In 1760 the presidio buildings of timber were rebuilt of stone, the walls were realigned into a quadrangle with four corner bastions, and a moat was dug all around the compound. The installation was renamed Real Presidio de San Saba. Warfare with the Comanche was now constant, yet the Spanish clung to the outpost so aggressively that rumors soon began to circulate of a rich silver mine in the area that they would not abandon. Conditions at the presidio were terrible. As supply trains were ambushed and livestock stolen by the Comanche, food shortages were commonplace, and soldiers wounded and sick suffered from the lack of proper medical supplies.

When a severe epidemic broke out at the presidio in 1768, the commanding officer could take no more. Without orders to do so he just marched the garrison away to San Antonio and abandoned the post. Though no troops were ever stationed there again, it was not until 1772 that the Real Presidio de San Saba was officially designated as abandoned by the Spanish authorities.

Later History

As the harsh Tejas weather slowly destroyed the empty presidio, stories of the now lost silver mine and its vast riches persisted.

In 1831 James and Rezin Bowie led an eleven-man expedition out of San Antonio bound for the San Saba River area. It was rumored and later stated in a written account by one of the expedition participants that Rezin had located the silver mine in 1829, and the brothers were now on their way to claim the treasure. As the small group of men, two of whom were actually servants, approached the San Saba River, they became aware that they were being shadowed by a war party made up of Tawakonis, Wacos, and Caddos 164 strong. Realizing that to be caught in open territory would be fatal, the Bowie expedition tried to hurry along and make it to the crumbling presidio. Some six to twelve miles from the protection of the stone walls of the presidio, time ran out for the white men.

As the Indians moved to encircle and attack, the group raced to a stand of oak trees. Piling up rocks, branches, packs, and saddles, the men set up a defensive perimeter within the shelter of the trees and prepared to fight for their lives. For twelve brutal hours they repulsed attack after attack, surviving even a fire set to drive them from cover that burned away most of the underbrush around them. One man was killed, three were wounded, several horses were shot, and six pack mules ran away, but when the next day dawned they were still full of fight.

But no fight materialized. The warriors had suffered fifty-two dead the previous day and had decided that the price was too high to renew the attack. They withdrew in defeat. Many days later the Bowies and their companions, battered and bloody but alive, staggered back into San Antonio, never to return to the San Saba area again. Carved into the gateway of the San Saba presidio was left the inscription "Bowie con sua tropa" (Bowie and his men), and the mystery of the lost San Saba silver mine remains to this day.

Spanish Presidio Period

In 1936 part of the presidio was rebuilt using an 1846 inaccurate written description of the ruins. Today the remains of Real Presidio de San Saba stand in a county park two miles west of Menard off U.S. 190.

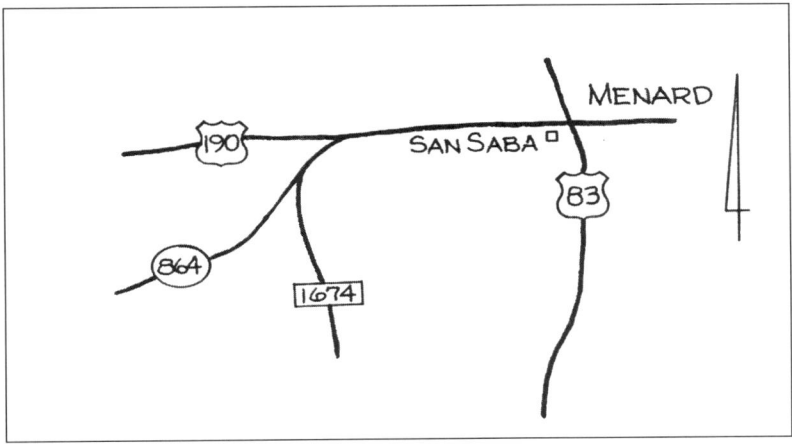

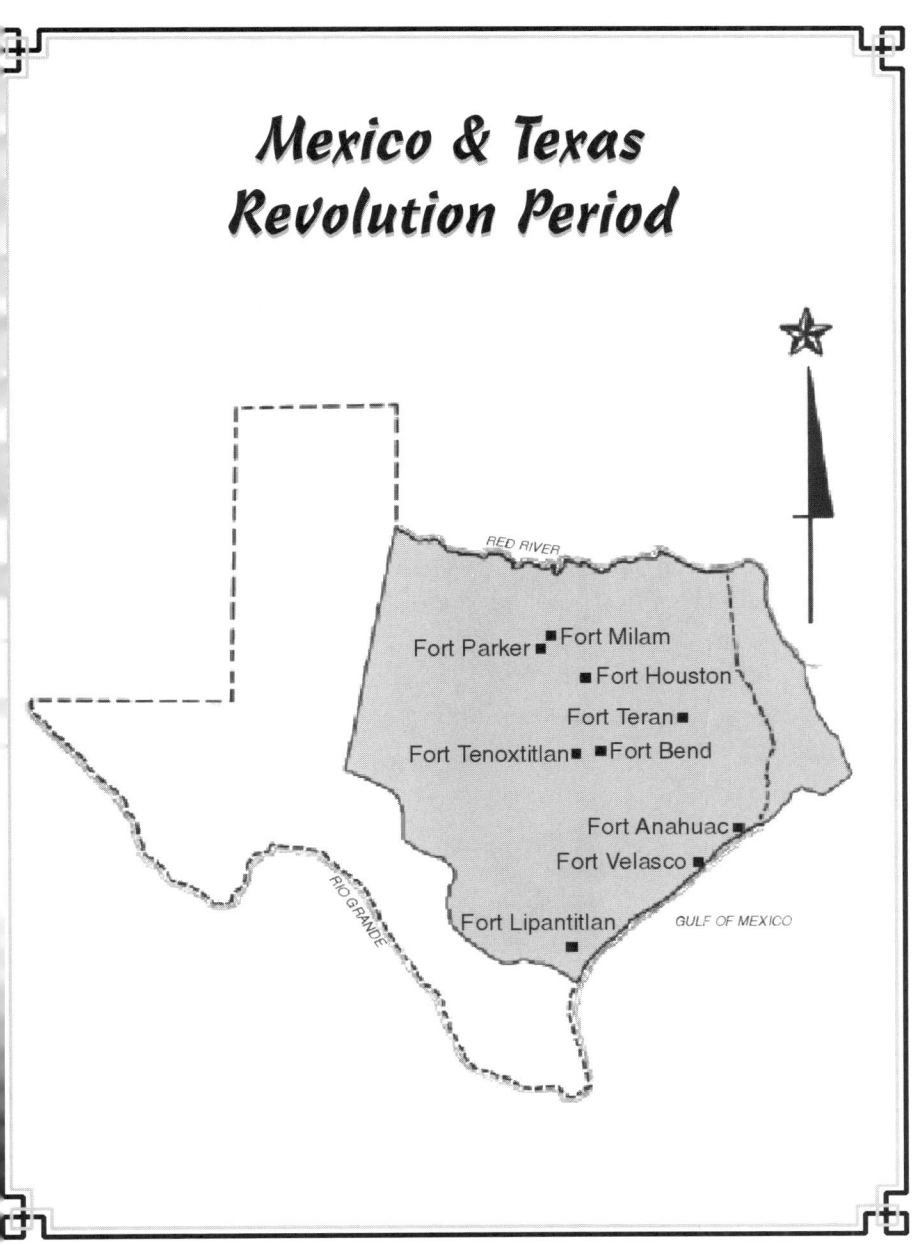

Alarmed by the continued influx of Americans into their Tejas province in the 1830s, Mexican authorities under the leadership of Antonio Lopez de Santa Anna enacted new laws and stationed troops at various points to stem the tide of immigration. One such military outpost so incensed the Tejas colonists that it later earned the name "Birthplace of the Texas Revolution."

Fort Anahuac

In November of 1830 Col. Juan Bradburn arrived at the mouth of the Trinity River commanding a column of 160 Mexican soldiers. His orders were to build and garrison a small fort that was to be used as a customhouse to collect taxes from traders sailing up and down the river. The fort, constructed on a bluff overlooking the river known as Perry's Point, was of great strategic, political, and economic value because it controlled the flow of goods to and from the colonists.

Mexico & Texas Revolution Period

The Mexican garrison lived in a fortified wooden barrack a half mile north of the construction site. The convict-soldiers, serving time in the army instead of prison, labored to make bricks for the fort's construction. Bradburn even conscripted local civilians and building materials for this work, a move that earned him the hatred of many colonists. He also began collecting import and export taxes on goods passing through his area of command. Worse still, escaped black slaves who sought protection with the Mexican military—slavery was illegal in Mexico—were pressed into service as laborers over the objections of bounty hunters and former masters seeking the return of the runaways.

Fort Anahuac began to take shape, even as the colonists' anger grew at the treatment received from Bradburn and his soldiers. The brick outer walls were more than seven feet thick, enclosing an area of one hundred feet by seventy feet. Two redoubts, at the northeast and southwest corners, commanded approaches by land and sea and were armed with one eighteen-pound pivot gun apiece. Inside the compound stood a reinforced brick building, fifty feet by thirty-five feet in size with walls four feet thick and two bulwarks, near the brick firing kilns, that were station for a sixteen-pound cannon each. An underground passage led from the fort to a powder magazine dug into a hillside forty yards from the walls.

In the nearby town of Anahuac, a local lawyer became the most strident agitator against Mexican policies and Col. Juan Bradburn in particular. His name was William Barret Travis. Bradburn hated Travis with a passion, viewing him as the leader of all opposition to his authority. Seizing on a minor incident, actually no more than a practical joke that may or may not have involved the young lawyer, Bradburn had Travis arrested and held prisoner inside the fort.

Armed colonists confronted Bradburn at Fort Anahuac, demanding the release of Travis and a fellow prisoner, Patrick C. Jack. Bradburn refused and threatened to kill his hostages, but he was later ordered to free the prisoners when the colonists took the matter to higher military authorities.

In 1832 Fort Anahuac was abruptly ordered abandoned, and the infamous Col. Bradburn had to sneak away in the dead of night to avoid the colonists' wrath. The departing troops dismantled as much of the brickwork as they could before leaving, and two fires after the fort was abandoned finished off any remaining wooden structures. Residents of Anahuac helped themselves to any unbroken bricks they

Mexico & Texas Revolution Period

could salvage from the site. But strangely, in January of 1835 the Mexicans sent a small force back to Fort Anahuac to rebuild and regarrison it. Locals set fire to all the building supplies and materials sent to the troops at the fort, which slowed down any reconstruction efforts. A force of Texian volunteers, under the leadership of none other than William Barret Travis, advanced on the Mexicans in June and demanded their immediate surrender. Travis spiced up his surrender demand with the threat of no quarter if the Mexicans chose to resist, a situation he would face himself in less than a year as commander of the Alamo. After the Mexican commander of Fort Anahuac complied, the garrison of forty soldiers were allowed to depart unmolested. The fort site was never used again.

Later History

The site of Fort Anahuac became private property, and nobody paid much attention to the ruins except as a local eyesore. A 1938 field survey noted the locations of the remaining foundations, and sometime after that rechanneling of the Trinity River washed away the ruins of the southwest redoubt. Chambers County bought the site in 1946 and cleared the land for use as a public park. All remaining rubble from Fort Anahuac was buried in place to provide for public safety. In the 1960s the Southwestern Historical Exploration Society of Houston conducted some excavations at the site, but vandalism caused the reburial of the work to protect the discoveries from malicious damage. A 1977 magnetometer survey of the site by the Texas Historical Commission revealed that 75 percent of the area had been previously disturbed in some way or other.

Fort Anahuac Park, located one mile south of the center of Anahuac just off State Highway 564, offers picnicking facilities, camping, restrooms, and a boat ramp. Several historic markers can be found in the park area that give a brief outline of the fort's location, configuration, and history.

Fort Velasco

Situated on the east side of the Brazos River at the Gulf of Mexico, the fort was built in 1831 to help the customs collector monitor shipping commerce on the river. Using driftwood logs placed upright in two rows, between which sand was packed, a circular enclosure 300 feet wide was constructed. Two large log buildings were erected inside, most of the common soldiers occupied two rows of tents, and a pile of earth

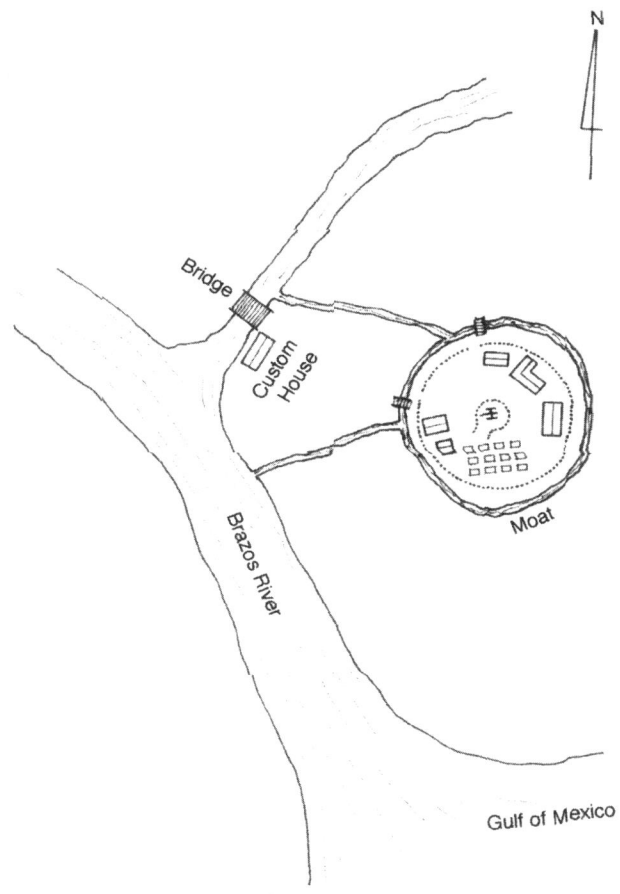

and sand was placed in the center of the fort. Standing over eight feet high and held in place by upright logs, this pile of sand was the position of the fort's single cannon. Able to fire over the walls and mounted on a swivel, the nine-pounder could be fired in any direction.

In 1832, when trouble broke out at Fort Anahuac over the arrest of William Barret Travis, armed colonists sailed down the Brazos River on the schooner *Brazoria* on their way to join the confrontation at Anahuac. The *Brazoria* was armed with two small cannons. Along the eastern riverbank, other colonists marched toward Fort Velasco. When the *Brazoria* sailed to within range of the fort's cannon, the post commander sent word that the ship would not be allowed to pass. The colonists decided that their forces on shore would attack the fort the next day, June 26, and the *Brazoria* dropped anchor below the fort to lend support.

Just after midnight the colonist forces began to creep toward Fort Velasco, hoping to surprise and overwhelm the garrison at sunrise. In the inky darkness someone accidentally discharged his musket, alerting the Mexicans. Heavy firing commenced from both sides, the fort's cannon blasting away at the *Brazoria* and the ship's cannons blasting right back. Luckily for the attackers on the ground, the fort's cannon could not be depressed to cover the area surrounding the walls, but small arms fire did much damage to their ranks.

Just after dawn, his ammunition running low, the Mexican commander surrendered his post. Seven colonists had been killed and five Mexican soldiers had died. The *Brazoria* became a transport ship, carrying the defeated Mexican garrison south to Matamoros. Fort Velasco was reoccupied by the Mexican army shortly thereafter, but no further trouble occurred there.

Mexico & Texas Revolution Period

After the Texas Revolution, the town of Velasco was the temporary capital of the new republic. All government records were stored in Fort Velasco until the first official capital of Texas was established at Columbia. The town of Velasco became a favorite resort area between the Texas Revolution and the Civil War, but nothing was ever done to preserve the fort site.

During the Civil War, Confederate forces fortified the port at Velasco with eight cannon batteries in several locations. The soldiers used all the wood of Fort Velasco for firewood and salvaged every piece of metal on the site for use as ammunition for their cannons. Eventually, by 1887, a private residence was built on the site of the fort. The great hurricane of 1900 that destroyed Galveston also devastated the town of Velasco. The entire site was abandoned.

Later History

Several attempts to locate the exact site of Fort Velasco in the twentieth century met with varying degrees of success and failure. This was due, in part, to weather-related reconfiguration of the area and to other construction at the site over the years. Many artifacts, for instance, have been uncovered from the Civil War fortifications the Confederates constructed. Cannonballs unearthed in 1980 were classified as being from the Civil War era, but some local historians disputed the findings based on the small size of the ordnance and claimed they were actually from the fort's earlier time period. Adding to the confusion was a vast amount of excavated material dumped on the site from harbor dredging and the construction of a Coast Guard station and jetty.

The probable site of Fort Velasco was purchased by the Texas Gulf Coast Parks and Restoration Association and is located near the Surfside U.S. Coast Guard Station. The Brazoria County Historical Museum in Angleton can provide information on Fort Velasco and the battle fought there. The museum is located at 100 East Cedar Street, and its hours of operation are Monday through Friday 9 A.M. to 5 P.M. and Saturday 9 A.M. to 3 P.M.

To enforce the orders restricting further American immigration and protect the route north in east Tejas, a Mexican fort was hastily established that one observer dryly noted would have been better suited to be a hog pen.

Fort Lipantitlan

The fort, situated on the west bank of the Nueces River, was an earthen embankment enclosure lined with upright fence posts to hold the dirt in place, thrown together in 1831. Several wooden buildings, one a barracks, were constructed outside the fort. Fort Lipantitlan was garrisoned by poorly armed soldiers numbering between eighty and one hundred twenty men. At the onset of open hostilities between the residents of Tejas and the Mexican government—the Texas Revolution—the fort gained strategic value as a possible staging point for attacks into east Tejas. After the fall of Goliad to revolutionary forces in 1835, an expedition was sent from there to take control of Fort Lipantitlan.

A force of nearly seventy Texians fell upon the fort on November 4, 1835, burning the buildings and capturing twenty-seven soldiers and two cannon. To their dismay, the Texians discovered that the post commander had already left for Goliad with the majority of the garrison, intending to stage a raid of his own. The two forces had just missed each other. The Texians decided to return to Goliad at once, unaware that the commander of Fort Lipantitlan had changed his mind about a raid and had already turned his troops around to return to their base. This time the two groups ran right into each other while crossing the Nueces River, and the ensuing battle was a clear victory for the Texians. The victors

returned to Goliad without bothering to occupy Fort Lipantitlan, but neither was it reoccupied by Mexican troops.

After Texas won its independence, Mexican armies were routinely sent north to raid the new republic in areas of disputed ownership. The Army of the Republic of Texas was hard-pressed to thwart every incursion, and a policy of retaliatory raids into Mexico was instituted. Hearing that Texan forces were mustering at Fort Lipantitlan to conduct such a raid, Mexican military forces were hurried north to strike first. The Texan commander at the fort was alerted by scouts of the approaching Mexicans and managed to move his 192 men to a more defensible position 200 yards from the fort on a bluff along the Nueces River.

On the morning of July 7, 1842, the Mexican force attacked Fort Lipantitlan, finding it deserted except for a handful of Texans, who had returned to gather up items forgotten when the troops had relocated the day before. The infuriated Mexican commander located the Texans' new position and ordered his nearly 500 men to attack. Cavalry and infantry charges were easily repulsed, and cannon fire was ineffective. The Mexicans broke off their assault and withdrew to Fort Lipantitlan. The next day they packed up and headed back to Mexico.

After the Mexican War put an end to further incursions into Texas in the mid-1840s, Fort Lipantitlan was abandoned as a military outpost.

Later History

Today the site of Fort Lipantitlan is a five-acre state historic site established in 1937. No trace of the earthen embankments of the fort remain. In the mid-1980s archeological digs in and around the site yielded a wealth of artifacts and confirmed that the area was extensively traveled by Indians long before the white man came. Evidence of occupation from the Spanish, Mexican, and Texan periods included such diverse items as military buttons, weaponry, tools, hardware, and money.

Lipantitlan State Historic Site is located at the intersection of FM 624 and FM 70, north of Banquete.

Fort Tenoxtitlan

In June of 1830, 100 soldiers of the garrison of Bexar, members of the Alamo de Parras, were sent to establish a fort on the San Antonio Road where it crossed the Brazos River. Reaching their destination in July, the soldiers set up a temporary camp on the east bank of the river a half mile below the crossing while a suitable permanent fort site was sought. A bluff overlooking the river, twelve miles above the crossing, on the west bank was the site chosen by the unit commander, Lt. Col. Jose Francisco Ruiz. In October the garrison moved to the selected location and began construction of their fort.

Log cabins were built, surrounded by a stockade, and a nearby spring-fed creek was diverted to the site to provide fresh water. The fort was given the ancient Aztec name Tenoxtitlan, meaning "prickly pear." The garrison was under orders to turn back any Anglo immigrants, but Col. Ruiz was sympathetic to the colonists.

Shortly after the completion of Fort Tenoxtitlan, a group of fifty American families had arrived with a charter to colonize the area. Col. Ruiz sent a messenger to Coahuila, province headquarters, to ask for instructions on how to handle the situation. The reply, three months later, was that the charter was now invalid and the colonists were to be arrested and marched back to Nacogdoches, in eastern Tejas, under guard.

By now the American families had already spread out from Fort Tenoxtitlan, with the blessing of Ruiz, and were establishing their homesteads in the area. An American merchant had even been allowed to open a general store inside the fort and was carrying on a brisk trade with Mexican soldiers and local Indians. Unwilling to upset the harmony of the thriving farming community, Ruiz sent word back to Coahuila that the colonists had moved on before word reached him to detain them and he had no idea where they might be now.

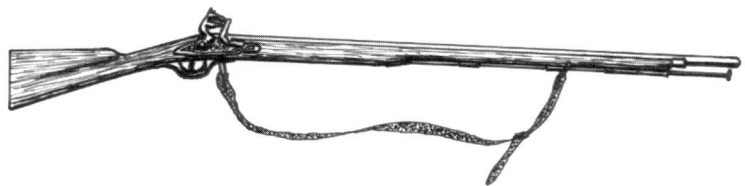

In 1832, after no communication or supplies had arrived from the Mexican government in some time, Ruiz took it upon himself to abandon Fort Tenoxtitlan and return to San Antonio. He probably believed that the government had forgotten about him, and he also was aware that the purpose of the fort had not been served under his command. Newly arrived colonists moved into the fort's log cabins and made them their new homes.

The old fort site served briefly as a supply depot and mustering point against raiding Indians for a few years after the Texas Revolution. It was abandoned in 1841 and by 1860 had completely disappeared.

Later History

In 1936 a granite marker was placed at the former site of Fort Tenoxtitlan by the Texas Centennial Commission. The site is fourteen miles northeast of Caldwell off Farm Road 1362.

The Burleson County Historical Museum in Caldwell displays exhibits about Fort Tenoxtitlan and its commander, Jose Francisco Ruiz, who would be a signer of the Texas Declaration of Independence in 1836. The museum, housed in the Burleson County Courthouse, is open on Fridays from 2 P.M. to 4:30 P.M.

Fort Teran

Completed in April of 1832, the fort was located on the Neches River where three major trails—the Coushatta Trace, Alabama Trace, and Nacogdoches-Orcoquisac Road—crossed the river. Charged with halting any further immigration into Tejas, the garrison was housed in ten wooden cabins. No real fort was ever constructed. Most of the troops there were reassigned in 1834, and the fort site was taken over by American settlers.

A trading post operated out of one of the buildings, and a post office was set up from 1856 to 1866. The small community nearby was sometimes referred to as Fort Turan.

The site of Fort Teran is on the Neches River, half a mile south of Shawnee Creek and three miles west of Rockland. Two historical markers at the site are not accessible without a 4-wheel-drive vehicle.

Fort Bend

In 1821 members of the colony of San Felipe de Austin—William Smithers, Joseph Polley, William Little, Henry Holster, and Charles Beard—built a wooden blockhouse near a large bend in the Brazos River. The site, on the west bank of the river, was chosen by Stephen F. Austin to guard the ford located there and protect the area from Indian raids, assuring the safety of his colony. A small community soon grew up near the crossing and blockhouse.

During the Texas Revolution of 1836, a rearguard action was fought at Fort Bend. A small Texian force attempted to halt or slow down the advancing Mexican army as it pursued

Sam Houston and the retreating revolutionary army during what was called the "Runaway Scrape." The Mexican juggernaut rolled right through Fort Bend and the Brazos River crossing without breaking stride.

After the stunning victory of Houston's army at San Jacinto in April of 1836, the blockhouse was briefly occupied by Texian forces as they followed the Mexican retreat from Texas. But with peace there was no longer a pressing need to protect the river crossing, and the blockhouse was allowed to deteriorate until it crumbled into a pile of rotting logs.

In 1833 a group of religious families, led by Elder Daniel Parker and calling themselves the Predestinarian Baptist Church, left Illinois and headed for Tejas.

Fort Parker

When the ox-drawn caravan of wagons reached a location within their land grant that suited Parker, they halted and began to build an enclosed community. A large stockade was erected of split cedars, twelve feet in height, around two rows of log cabins and two two-story blockhouses on opposite corners of the rectangular enclosure. Fields nearby were cleared for planting, and by March of 1834 all the families who had elected to stay with Parker (others had previously decided to move on and settle further west on the Navasota River) were quartered inside the fort.

The residents of Fort Parker included the family of Daniel Parker, the families of his brothers Silas, James, and Benjamin, and their father, John. Also part of the community were the Kellogg, Nixon, Frost, Plummer, and Duty families. The settlement prospered until the morning of May 19, 1836.

Most of the men and some women were out of the fort tending the fields of crops when a large band of Caddo and Comanche Indians rode toward Parker's Fort from the east, the rider in the lead carrying a white flag. Benjamin Parker, one of the few men at the fort that morning, went to speak with the warriors when they reined up in front of the gates. He returned in a short while with word that the Indians had only asked for some beef and for permission to camp nearby. A potentially deadly situation seemed to have been averted.

Mexico & Texas Revolution Period

But when Parker stepped through the gates with the requested beef, he was immediately run through with a lance. The warriors charged the gates before the startled settlers could push them closed. Moving through the compound with terrible ferocity, the warriors killed John and Silas Parker, Samuel and Robert Frost, and many others. They captured Elizabeth Kellogg, Rachael Plummer, her son James, and the children of Silas Parker, John and Cynthia Ann. The workers in the fields, hearing the sounds of carnage, hid themselves until the Indians had finished looting the fort and had left, carrying away their captives. After dark, the survivors split up into two groups and made their way toward Fort Houston, sixty miles away.

Cynthia Ann Parker was nine years old when she was taken captive. She was adopted into the Pahuka band of the Comanche tribe and over the years gradually became more Indian than white. Becoming the wife of Chief Peta Nacona in her teens, she bore him three children. One of her sons would become the last great chief of the Comanche, Quanah Parker.

Later History

In 1933 private owners deeded the land where Fort Parker had once stood, long since abandoned and decayed, to the state of Texas. A replica of the fort was constructed at the site as part of the 1936 Texas Centennial celebration. In 1967 a new replica was built after the first one fell into disrepair. The Old Fort Parker State Historic Site encompasses 37.5 acres and features picnic and camping areas, a dining pavilion, restrooms, and showers.

The Fort Parker site is located eleven miles south of Mexia, one mile off State Highway 14 on Park Road 35.

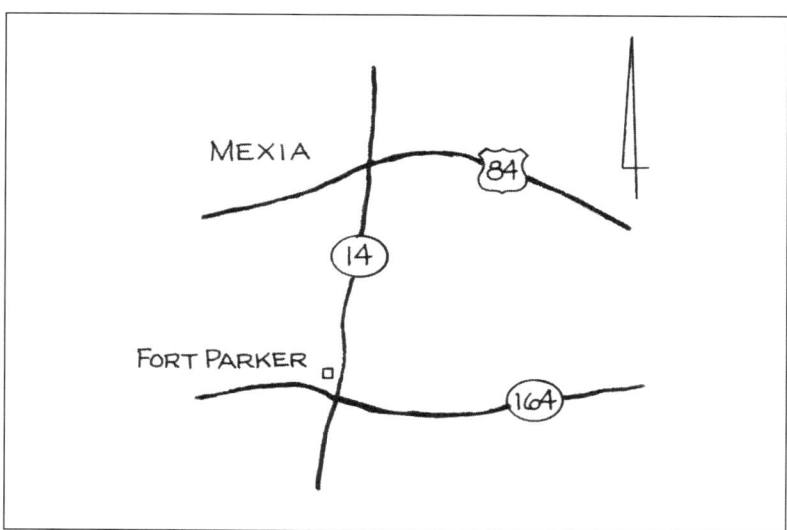

Fort Lacy

Originally a home and trading post built in 1835 by Martin Lacy in eastern Tejas, it was built near the present-day town of Alto. In 1838, during an uprising of the local Kickapoo and Biloxi Indians, Lacy abandoned the site in favor of another homestead forty-five miles southwest. He returned after things had quieted down and began to fortify the first site by constructing a log blockhouse and an encircling stockade wall.

In 1839 the fort was used as a staging and supply area for militiamen and volunteers on a campaign to drive the Indians from eastern Texas entirely. The campaign lasted for more than a year and resulted in the expulsion of most tribes from the region, friendly or not. In 1840 Fort Lacy housed a unit of regular army troops passing through on their way to a duty assignment further west.

By 1841 Fort Lacy had outlived its usefulness and was dismantled by Lacy himself.

Tumlinson Fort

Built on the headwaters of Brushy Creek by a company of rangers in early 1836, the single-story wooden blockhouse was named for the company commander, Capt. John Tumlinson. The post was originally manned by a force of sixty men; their orders were to patrol the region and protect local settlers. When news reached the garrison of the Mexican army advancing into Tejas to put down the revolution, the men abandoned the post to go fight the invaders.

In 1837 the entire post was burned to the ground by marauding Comanches.

Fort Houston

Constructed in early 1836 on the public square of the town of Houston, the fort consisted of a stockade and wooden blockhouse. Built by a company of Texas Rangers from the area at the orders of Gen. Sam Houston as a protection against Indians, the fort stockade covered an acre of ground and the blockhouse measured twenty-five square feet.

Fort Houston was never attacked, but townspeople often spent the night in the blockhouse as a precaution. The fort was abandoned in 1841, and the town of Houston went into decline, ceasing to exist when the nearby town of Palestine became the Anderson County seat in 1846.

In 1857, 600 acres of land in the area, including the sites of the fort and town, passed into the private ownership of Texas statesman John H. Reagan. The home he built there became known as Fort Houston. A state historical marker was placed at the site in 1936, two miles south of Palestine off U.S. 79S on FM 1990.

Fort Milam

Built on the west bank of the Brazos River in 1834, the installation was first called Fort Viesca. In December of 1835 it was renamed in honor of Ben Milam, who had died leading the assault on San Antonio de Bexar. In 1836 the fort was abandoned during the Runaway Scrape.

After independence, the fort was reoccupied by units of the Texas Rangers, under the leadership of Col. Edward Burleson, and remained a ranger outpost until the late summer of 1837, when it was abandoned. Rangers from Fort Milam constructed and garrisoned the Little River Fort and Fort Fisher. Fort Milam was the first of two installations to be so named.

The site is marked by a stone monument located four miles southwest of the town of Mexia.

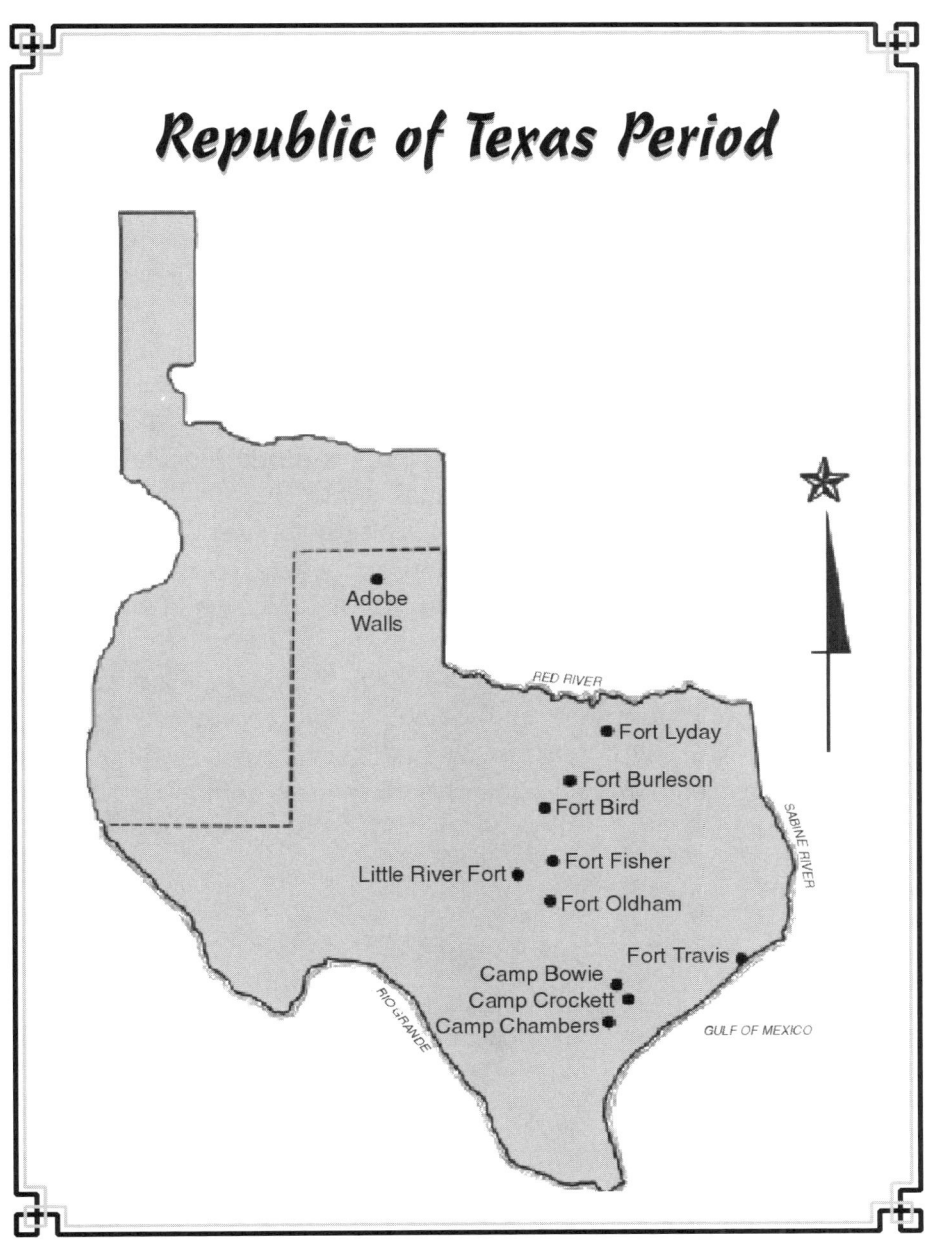

Typical Family Fort

The most untypical of frontier fortifications, the family fort was not a military outpost but, as the name implies, a civilian one. In isolated areas several families or individuals would band together for common defense. The method they used was to either strengthen and fortify a single home or construct an enclosed complex containing many dwellings.

Commonly, a group of cabins would be built together and surrounded by a stockade wall. Where wood was scarce, adobe bricks would be used. Sometimes raised blockhouses would be added. Residents would either occupy the compound or retreat there, if possible, during times of trouble with the local Indians. Ample supplies would be stockpiled there for the people to live off of until the danger had passed and it was safe to venture out again.

The use of family forts on the Texas frontier was a necessity in areas unprotected by regular military patrols and nearby forts. The family fort insured safety and survival in a harsh environment and strengthened the ties of independent communities.

Fort Lyday

Situated a half mile north of the North Sulphur River on the property of Isaac Lyday in 1836, the "family fort" consisted of ten-by-twelve-foot buildings surrounded by a picket wall. In the center of the quarter-acre compound, a large well was situated to supply water for the inhabitants. Living quarters were located along the inside of the east, west, and south walls, while along the north wall the buildings were used as storerooms. Just outside the stockade a livestock corral was erected. Several families were able to use the fort as protection from Indian raiders.

In 1838 a unit of Texas Rangers was organized locally and moved into the nearly abandoned compound. Under the direction of newly elected Captain Isaac Lyday, many improvements were made to the fort's defenses by the rangers. Fourteen new families were brought into the fort when Indian raids increased in the region. After that time the fort saw only limited use as people drifted back to their own homesteads when the Indian threat subsided.

By 1843 the need for the fort had all but vanished and the last occupants had moved out. The fort was used as an occasional temporary shelter by many locals until it was allowed to fall into disrepair. After the Civil War Fort Lyday had disappeared entirely.

Fort Oldham

This was a fortified house constructed by William Oldham on his property west of the Brazos River in 1836-37. Settlers from the area took refuge at the fort during periods of Indian raids, and by 1838 a post office had been established there.

By 1841 the fort was officially designated as a station on the post office route between the towns of Independence and Franklin. The site of the house is on property still owned by Oldham's descendants.

As the infant Republic of Texas took its first tottering steps toward maturity, it soon had to deal with a major problem inherited from the Spanish and Mexicans. The problem was the Indians.

Fort Fisher

Settlers began to spread out over the fertile areas of the new country almost as soon as the last shots of the revolution were fired. The Brazos River valley became a prime destination, an isolated area populated by Waco tribes and the raiding grounds of Comanche and Kiowa warriors. After several bloody incidents near the sites of modern Waco and Mexia, the government decided to station a company of "rangers" in the contested territory.

In 1837 a detachment of forty-five men established Fort Fisher on the site of an old Waco village near the Brazos River. Consisting of nothing more than a few tents and crudely constructed wooden shanties, the fort served only briefly as a base of operations to protect arriving settlers. Though it was an attractive campsite, nearby artesian springs providing abundant fresh water, the post was not situated to provide the rapid response to Indian threats needed at that time. Fort Fisher was abandoned soon after it was established.

Had it not been for the legend surrounding the men (and those who followed in their footsteps) of the original garrison, Fort Fisher might have faded into obscurity. But those men were Texas Rangers.

Today the fort constructed in 1968 south and east of the original location bears no resemblance to the first installation. Situated in a 35-acre park in Waco, the fort shares its location with The Texas Ranger Hall of Fame. In the museum are displays of Texas Ranger history that include guns and weapons, Indian items, personal histories of famous rangers, and western art. The park provides a reproduction of a frontier fort the original garrison would have envied. There are paid camping and picnic sites available.

Located just off I-35 at Lake Brazos and University Park Drives, the museum is open daily from 9 A.M. to 5 P.M. and admission is charged.

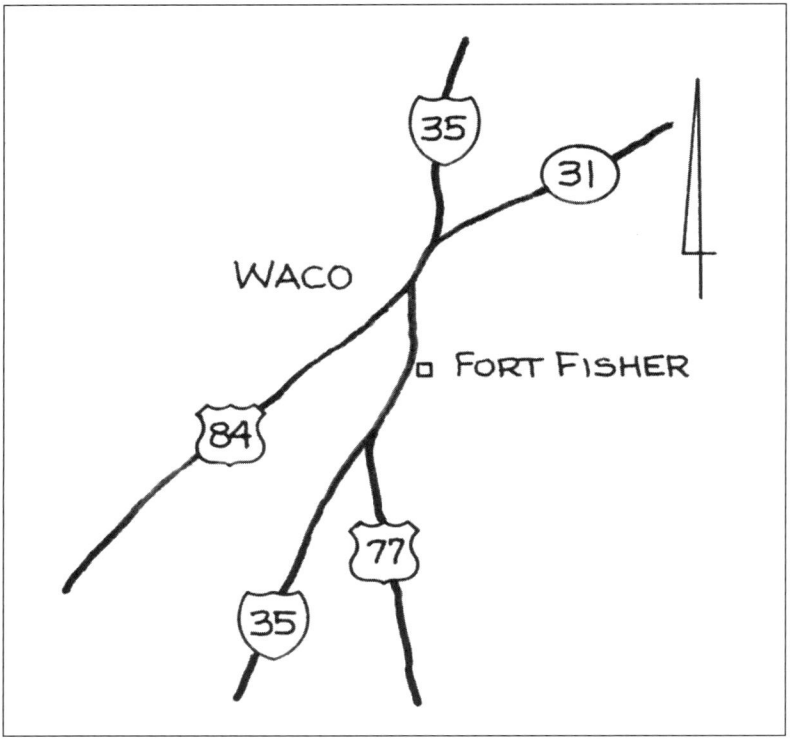

The largest battle fought between Indians and soldiers during the Civil War took place at the site of a former trading post in the Texas Panhandle. Ten years later another battle would be fought nearby between Indians and buffalo hunters. Both battles would be known by the same name, taken from a site that had its beginnings while Texas was a republic.

Adobe Walls

This site was established in 1843 just north of the Canadian River in Texas by the firm of Bent, St. Vrain, and Company because Comanches and Kiowas would not trade at Bent's Fort in Colorado. The close proximity of their enemies, the Cheyenne and Arapaho, kept them away. The traders decided to bring their merchandise to the consumer and set up a trading post in the territory controlled by the Comanche and Kiowa. Working first from tepees and later from a log fort, company traders carried on a brisk business in this new market.

Around 1846 the company sent a large number of Mexican adobe makers to replace the log fort with a brick one. The resulting Fort Adobe was a box-like enclosure eighty feet square with only one entrance. Several buildings were constructed behind the nine-foot walls. Unfortunately, relations with the local tribes became strained, brought on perhaps by the hostile attitude of nearby Apaches, and the fort was abandoned in 1848, along with all attempts to trade in the region.

One effort was made to reopen Fort Adobe in 1849 that ended in failure when the wagon train carrying goods was attacked and a few head of livestock were stolen. The traders packed the interior of Fort Adobe with gunpowder and blew the place up. They returned to Colorado and never came back. The ruins they left behind became a local landmark known as Adobe Walls, after those portions of the fort that had not been toppled by the explosion. There the story might have ended.

First Battle of Adobe Walls

In November of 1864 Col. Christopher (Kit) Carson led elements of the 1st New Mexico Union Cavalry into the Canadian River area of Texas. His orders were to attack the winter camps of the Comanche and Kiowa who had been raiding wagon trains on their way to and from Santa Fe. At the head of a column of infantry and cavalry numbering over 300 men, two mountain howitzers, and a twenty-seven-wagon supply train, Carson led the way toward Adobe Walls.

When his scouts reported many villages in the vicinity of Adobe Walls, Carson pushed on ahead with his cavalry and the howitzers, leaving his infantry to guard the supply train and follow later. His first target was a sleeping Kiowa village of about 150 lodges, which he attacked and burned in the early morning. The Kiowas scattered to the other villages nearby to spread the alarm while Carson and his men pushed rapidly on to Adobe Walls.

Setting up a defensive position in one corner of the ruins, his howitzers placed on a nearby rise, Carson was besieged by between 3,000 and 7,000 Kiowa and Comanche warriors. This was far greater opposition than he had expected, and throughout the day assault after assault was repulsed, the howitzers doing deadly work on the mounted attacking warriors. The soldiers within the ruins actually managed to mount a few counterattacks under cover of the big guns.

As the day wore on and ammunition began to run low, Carson began to fear for the fate of his slow-moving supply train and the infantry escort. Conducting an orderly withdrawal from Adobe Walls, under the cover of his howitzers, Carson and his men fought their way through the encircling warriors, managing to set fire to other villages on the way, and made their way back to the unmolested supply train. Now Carson determined he had done all the damage he could and that it was time to return to New Mexico. As the expedition headed for home, they left behind almost two hundred burned lodges, one hundred fifty dead warriors, and an untold amount of destroyed Indian winter supplies. They carried away with them three dead and twenty-five wounded of their own.

Second Battle of Adobe Walls

In the 1870s the decimation of the buffalo herds of the West began in earnest. Buffalo hunters, with their powerful rifles, would bring wholesale slaughter to the plains for $3.50 a hide. They would also help end the free-roaming lifestyle of the Indians who lived off the buffalo herds.

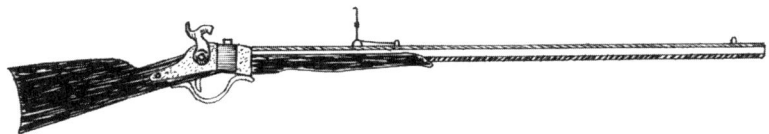

In the spring of 1874, a group of buffalo hunters set up a camp near a trading post that consisted of four buildings constructed of cut sod slabs, a mile or so away from the old ruins of Adobe Walls, and a corral. When about 700 Comanche and Kiowa warriors rode down on the trading post and camp, seeking to defend their territory and kill the invaders, there were only twenty-nine whites there: twenty-eight men and one woman. Included in the group were two men destined for fame, one later and one as a result of the upcoming fight. The former was a twenty-year-old Canadian named Bartholomew Masterson, who would later become a western legend known as Bat Masterson, and the latter was twenty-three-year-old Billy Dixon.

Most of the hunters were awake when the shouting warriors, under the leadership of Comanche chief Quanah Parker, roared down on them in the early morning of June 27, 1874. Two men and a dog were lost in the first onslaught as they raced for cover in the sturdy sod buildings. The initial charge swirled around the structures, but the hunters and merchants were well protected and poured a deadly fire into the attackers. The warriors withdrew, regrouped, and charged again and again, some even backing their horses into the doors in an attempt to knock them down.

Throughout the day the attacks continued, the intervals between them growing longer and longer. The hunters lost another man killed while the warriors lost around thirty. Toward mid-afternoon Quanah Parker decided that the cost of continuing the assaults would be too high in lives lost, and he broke off the fight. Releasing most of the warriors to return home or raid elsewhere, the chief left a large enough force on the hills and ridges around the buildings to watch for an opportunity to finish the hunters off. Hesitantly, the besieged whites began to leave the buildings and survey the scene of the battle. The warriors watched intently from hiding nearby.

Neither side even noticed the approach of a group of riders from the north. Unaware that a battle had just taken place and miraculously missing contact with bands of scattering warriors, another group of buffalo hunters arrived.

The next morning Billy Dixon became famous. Twelve mounted warriors were spotted on a bluff about one mile east of the compound, probably trying to estimate the odds of a successful attack now that reinforcements had come in to bolster the buffalo hunters' numbers. Dixon steadied his Sharps rifle, a single-shot breechloader that fired a 550-grain .50-caliber slug, took careful aim, and squeezed off a round in the direction of the distant warriors. As the smoke cleared and the sound of the report faded away into the distance, everyone assumed Dixon's shot had fallen short. Suddenly, one of the warriors jerked convulsively and toppled from his horse. That was it for the Indians; they packed up and left the area immediately. One more defender died when he accidentally shot himself while climbing down from a rooftop where he had been watching the warriors departing. Later Dixon's shot was measured at 1,538 yards, or 7/8 of a mile, and became known as the Mile-Long Shot.

Later History

Hunters, merchants, and settlers abandoned the area of Adobe Walls after the 1874 fight, but in the early 1880s Billy Dixon returned to the ruins of the old fort and built a house there. He and several other men nearby ranched the area of Adobe Walls. Dixon served as postmaster until 1901, operating the local post office from his home until he moved in 1902. In 1920 the local school occupied the second floor of the old Dixon place until a new schoolhouse could be built to replace a recently burned one. The first-floor post office was closed in 1921.

The Panhandle-Plains Historical Society purchased the site of the second Battle of Adobe Walls and six acres around it in 1923, erecting a plaque to commemorate the battle.

The site of the first Battle of Adobe Walls, the old fort location, is on private property, but a state historical marker is located five miles north of Stinnett at the junction of State Highway 207 and FM 136. The site of the second Battle of Adobe Walls is on the Turkey Track Ranch, about one and a half miles south of the ranch main building. A state historical marker at the intersection of State Highway 15 and FM 278 nearby, also north of Stinnett, makes mention of both battles.

Two museums in the area deal with the battles of Adobe Walls. The West Texas A&M University Museum in Canyon and the Hutchinson County Historical Museum in Borger display information and artifacts of both battles.

Fort Bird

Constructed by volunteers from the 4th Brigade of Texas Militia in 1841 to protect the extreme northeast corner of the Texas frontier, the fort consisted of a large blockhouse and several smaller log buildings surrounded by a stockade. Situated on the Trinity River, in the vicinity of present-day Fort Worth, the fort was abandoned in August of 1843. In September of that year, a council between nine local Indian tribes and representatives of the Republic of Texas was held at the fort. The treaty they hammered out ended existing hostilities and established a clear boundary between the white settlements and Indian territory. After that the fort remained unused and eventually disappeared.

Fort Travis

Established on the eastern end of Galveston Island in 1836, it was used to protect the Galveston harbor entrance. The earthen fort was octagonal in shape and mounted with six- and twelve-pound naval cannon. This was the first installation named for Alamo commander William Barret Travis. The fort was abandoned in 1844, and no trace of it exists today.

Camp Bowie

The primary encampment of the Army of the Republic of Texas after independence from Mexico was won was located on the east side of the Navidad River at Red Bluff, one mile below Texana. The camp was only occupied from April to June of 1837. A succession of camp commanders failed to instill in the rowdy troops a sense of discipline and military protocol.

When a colonel was murdered at Camp Bowie in May of 1837, President Sam Houston ordered furloughs and transfers for most of the soldiers stationed there. The last 200 men at the camp in June were all transferred to nearby Camp Crockett, and Camp Bowie, named for Alamo defender Jim Bowie, was abandoned.

Camp Crockett

Camp Crockett, named for Alamo defender David Crockett, became the main encampment and headquarters for what remained of the Army of the Republic of Texas after the near mutinous events at Camp Bowie in May of 1837. Situated on the Navidad River, Camp Crockett was home to the least troublesome of the soldiers from the previous camp; the rest had been furloughed indefinitely. Within two months of their arrival, the troops were again transferred, and Camp Crockett was abandoned.

Camp Chambers

The last permanent encampment of the dwindling Army of the Republic of Texas, the camp was located on the west bank of Arenosa Creek near the Texana-Victoria Road crossing. Troops from Camp Crockett arrived in August of 1837 and were released from duty there in October and November. Camp Chambers was then abandoned.

Fort Sherman

Established a mile north of Cypress Creek in 1838 as a protection for settlers living in the area and manned by local militia, it was in use until the 1840s. When the Cherokee Indians were finally driven out of East Texas, the fort was abandoned.

Little River Fort

The fort was built near the junction of the Leon and Lampasas Rivers in late 1836 by a company of Texas Rangers under the command of Capt. Thomas H. Barron. The fort, known as Little River Fort, Fort Smith, or Fort Griffin, covered half an acre. The stockade was nine feet high, enclosing a sixteen-foot-square blockhouse and seven log cabins.

In 1837 the rangers were withdrawn to garrison other posts, and the Little River Fort stood abandoned for over two years. A unit of the Army of the Republic of Texas was assigned to the fort in early 1840, but lack of supplies forced the soldiers to leave after only one month. The fort was regarrisoned later in the year but was abandoned in 1841, when the Army of the Republic was disbanded. Texas Rangers used the Little River Fort as a stopover point and handy shelter until 1846, as did many local travelers. Sometime after 1846 a gentleman named Moses Griffin took it upon himself to dismantle the entire fort by hand.

The site of Little River Fort is five miles southeast of Belton on FM 436.

Fort Burleson

It was originally called Fort Milam when it was built on the east bank of the Brazos River, a few miles from the first fort to bear that name, in February of 1839. The fort was roughly 150 square feet in size, its stockade walls rising to a height of eleven feet with bastions at each corner. Regulars of the Army of the Republic of Texas made up the garrison throughout the fort's brief history. In August of 1839 the name was officially changed to Fort Burleson, in honor of the commander of the army, Edward Burleson.

The garrison was reassigned to Camp Chambers in the spring of 1840, and the fort became the property of local citizens. Fort Burleson was maintained by area civilians as a place of protection against Indian attack. When the threat of

Indian raids had been eliminated, the fort was allowed to fall into disrepair. No trace of Fort Burleson remains.

Fort Colorado

Established on the north bank of the Colorado River just west of Walnut Creek in 1836, Fort Colorado was one in a series of frontier forts built by the new Republic of Texas to protect its citizens. Other forts in the chain included Little River Fort, Fort Houston, and Fort Milam.

Fort Colorado consisted of two two-story blockhouses and several log cabins enclosed by a high stockade wall. The fort was sometimes referred to as Fort Coleman, after the commander of the three companies of rangers garrisoning it, Col. Robert Coleman.

Within two years the rangers had aggressively quelled Indian activity in the region and provided local settlers with a relative sense of security in their homes. The fort was abandoned in 1838, and local civilians dismantled the post for its cut logs and lumber.

The former site of Fort Colorado today is located two and a half miles northeast of the Montopolis Bridge in Austin.

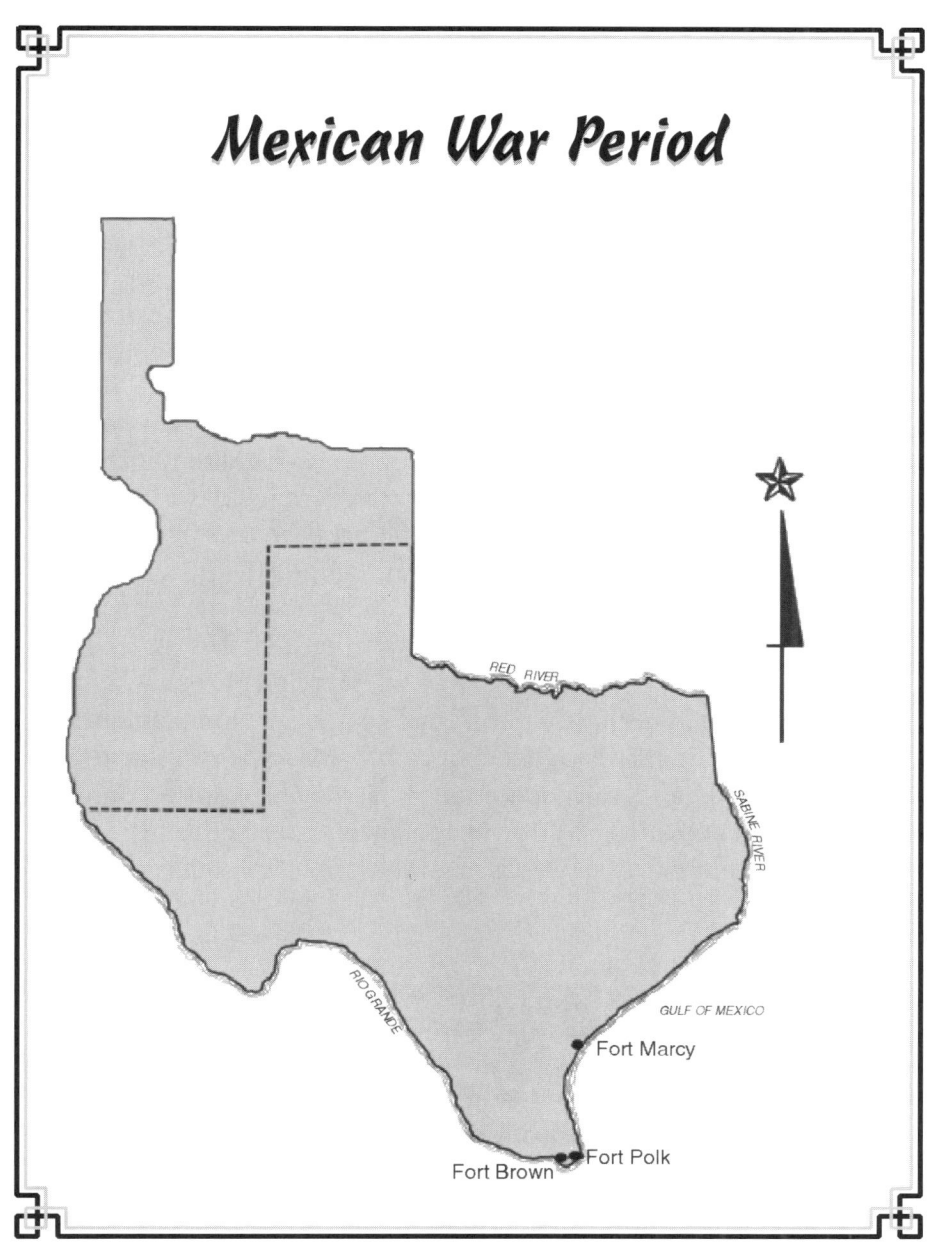

Fort Marcy

When Gen. Zachary Taylor brought his army into Texas in 1845, he set up a temporary post at Corpus Christi. This post, situated on the Gulf of Mexico, was the staging area for the eventual move south to the Rio Grande and the opening of armed conflict with Mexico. The name Fort Marcy was seldom used as a designation for the tent city the army occupied while awaiting orders to head south.

The site was abandoned in 1846, but a small garrison remained behind. In 1852 Fort Marcy was designated as the new army headquarters for Texas by the commander of military forces, Gen. Persifor F. Smith, because he preferred the climate of Corpus Christi over San Antonio. As the headquarters site it was also the main supply depot for all the forts in Texas, despite being far removed from the inland posts and thus creating longer transport time for supplies.

When Gen. Smith was transferred to another command in Kansas in 1856, the supply depot at Fort Marcy was immediately closed, and this operation was moved back to San Antonio along with the army headquarters. Despite its loss of importance, Fort Marcy was continuously garrisoned until 1881.

Later History

Today the Corpus Christi Army Depot is again in operation, being reactivated in 1961. It is the main helicopter repair and overhaul facility for the U.S. Army's fleet of air transport vehicles. The facility actually occupies the former site of the Corpus Christi Naval Air Station and not the original location of Fort Marcy.

The first U.S. Army fort ever constructed in Texas was built on the Rio Grande, opposite the town of Matamoros. The fort's presence, along with several other factors, helped bring about the war between the United States and Mexico.

Fort Texas

In 1846, 3,000 men of the U.S. Army marched south out of Corpus Christi and into the disputed area north of the Rio Grande claimed by both the Republic of Texas and Mexico. In March the army reached a bluff overlooking that river, across from Matamoros, and began to build a fortified enclosure there. Mexican soldiers in Matamoros immediately began construction of their own cannon emplacements and fortifications while regiments of troops arrived in the town. The dry tinder was now in place; all that remained was to strike flint to steel and make a spark.

The U.S. soldiers worked feverishly to erect their earthen fort. When completed it was in the shape of a six-pointed star, two sides 150 yards long and the remaining four sides 125 yards each. The angled walls of packed earth rose to a height of nine feet with a width of fifteen feet. Inside there were dug powder magazines and bomb shelters; cannon platforms were raised at each point of the star. Outside, a moat encircled the fort, twenty feet wide and eight feet deep, spanned by a single drawbridge. The fort was unofficially named Fort Texas when it was completed.

Satisfied that the defenses were the best that could be constructed in such a short time, General Zachery Taylor left a garrison under the command of Major Jacob Brown while he marched the rest of the army toward Port Isabel, site of Fort Polk. There, Taylor hoped to secure supplies for his army being landed by sea at the port. Across the Rio Grande, anxious eyes watched the U.S. soldiers depart.

The Mexicans began to bombard Fort Texas on May 3 from their emplacements across the river. The guns of the fort responded by lobbing a few shells back at Matamoros with such accuracy that many Mexican cannon were silenced. The Mexican army then crossed the Rio Grande en masse, leaving a large force to besiege and bombard Fort Texas and moving off in pursuit of Taylor's army. Seven Mexican cannon now pounded the fort at close range, while the defenders hunkered down to conserve ammunition and wait for reinforcements. Major Brown lost a leg to a cannonball early on in the siege.

Taylor, meanwhile, had heard the sound of the furious Mexican bombardment and had turned his army around to march back. On May 8 Taylor's troops met the pursuing Mexican army, some 4,000 strong, at Palo Alto. The daylong battle fought there was one of artillery and cavalry that resulted in an indecisive victory for the Americans when the Mexican army withdrew from the field in good order at dusk.

Taking up a defensive position at Resaca de la Palma, the Mexicans prepared to face the advancing Americans the next

Mexican War Period

day. This time, however, after some artillery fire and cavalry charges, Taylor threw his infantry forward against the Mexican cannon positions. He hoped to capture the enemy guns and remove them from any further role in the battle. In savage hand-to-hand fighting, the Americans seized the guns, breaking the lines of the Mexican infantry and routing them. The retreat this time was anything but orderly; the Mexican soldiers ran to the Rio Grande and swam across. Taylor's army now proceeded, unhindered, back to Fort Texas and broke the Mexican siege. Major Brown, one of only two fatalities at the fort, died just before his comrades arrived. On May 17 the fort was named in his honor.

Fort Brown

U.S. troops manned the fort for the remainder of the Mexican War. In 1848 construction of permanent quarters for officers and enlisted men was begun a quarter of a mile north of the original earthen fort. By 1852 a brick wall separated the new fort's buildings from the growing town of Brownsville, and the post was well on its way to becoming an important military station. On the 358-acre site were built accommodations and facilities for one battery of artillery, one company of cavalry, and four companies of infantry.

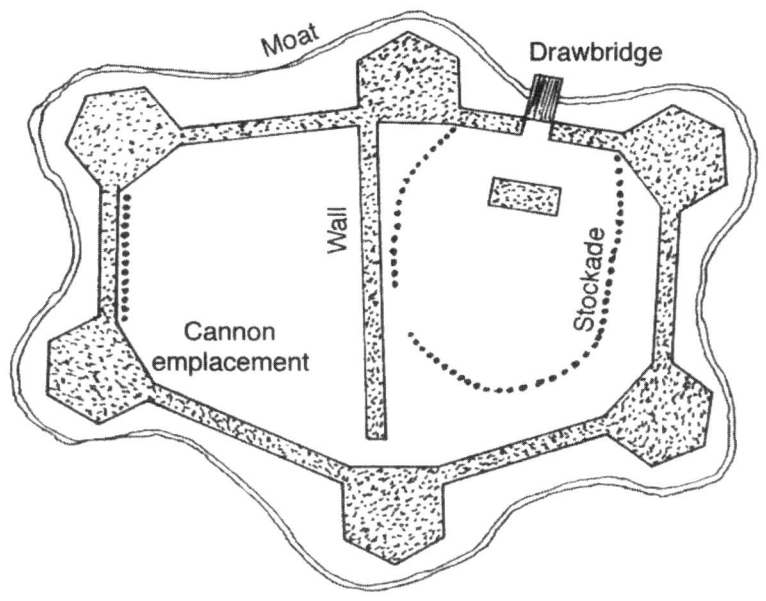

The fort was abandoned in 1861 and occupied by Confederate forces. In 1863 the Confederates were forced to retreat before a Union army advancing from Port Isabel. All the buildings were burned before the Federals could reclaim the fort. Less than a year later, in 1864, Fort Brown was attacked and retaken by the Confederates. They held the fort until the end of the war in 1865, when troops from Fort Brown took part in the last battle of the Civil War. At Palmito Ranch, Confederate forces turned back a Union force marching to occupy Brownsville, even though they were aware that Lee had surrendered two weeks earlier at Appomattox.

When the Federals took final possession of Fort Brown, a new building program was undertaken in 1869 that utilized brick construction wherever possible. The post commander's house was a one-and-a-half-story frame structure built on brick piers; the seven infantry officer's quarters nearby were of similar design. The cavalry barracks were built of brick while the four infantry barracks were two-story wooden structures. There were artillery quarters, a guardhouse, a post hospital, and a chapel constructed also. Fort Brown was a major installation for the remainder of its history, becoming a focal point in the efforts to curb Indian and Mexican bandit activities in the area. From 1906 to 1914 the fort was lightly garrisoned. At no time was any effort made to preserve the original Fort Brown, and the site gradually began to disappear.

Between 1914 and 1916 troops were poured into Fort Brown in response to border disturbances with Mexican bandits and revolutionaries. The fort became the headquarters of the 12th Cavalry regiment and remained so for the next nearly thirty years. Fort Brown was deactivated in 1944.

Later History

The city of Brownsville acquired the front 162 acres of Fort Brown in 1948. The post hospital was turned over to the school system for use by Texas Southmost Jr. College. Other buildings were sold or donated to local businesses and civic organizations. Some structures were relocated, others were torn down to make way for new construction, and the historical setting of Fort Brown totally disappeared.

Gone also is the original Fort Texas/Fort Brown. All that remains of the site now are grass-covered mounds, adjacent to a golf course, that indicate a faint outline of the fort. One area of the site is marked by an upended cannon barrel, installed in 1921, that is supposed to indicate the location of Major Brown's death in 1846. Additionally, there is a tabletop marker displaying the dimensions and location of the fort. More detailed information about Fort Brown, in all its incarnations, may be obtained at the Brownsville Visitors Information Center beside U.S. 77/83 at the FM 802 exit. The Fort Brown site itself is located at International Boulevard and May Street.

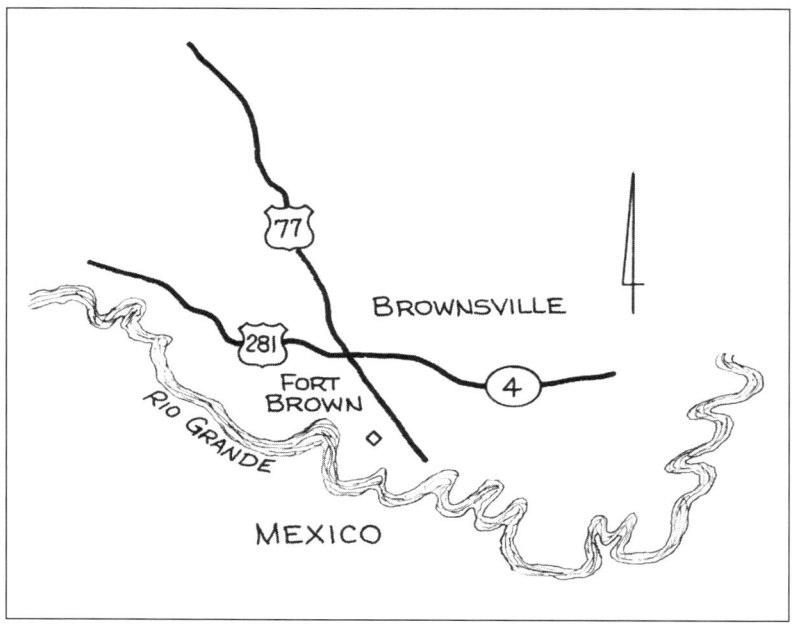

Fort Polk

Established in 1846, shortly after war with Mexico was declared, Fort Polk was situated on the Gulf of Mexico in extreme southern Texas as a supply depot for nearby Brownsville. The facility was actually a four-sided earthen enclosure with two sides that opened to the sea. Ships arriving with supplies for the American army would unload their cargo at Fort Polk, and from there it would be forwarded to the troops. The fort was abandoned in 1850, but the town of Port Isabel that was established close by continued to thrive on the shipping trade.

U.S. Army Period (1848-1861)

Typical U.S. Army fort

Army forts were primarily composed of buildings constructed around a large square or rectangular open area known as a parade ground. Usually, enlisted men's quarters, or barracks, were built on one side of the parade ground and officers' quarters on the opposite side. Other buildings, such as the commissary, hospital, and guardhouse were erected where space was available.

Behind the barracks were usually found the stables and storehouses, to allow the soldiers easy access to their horses and equipment. In most, but not all, cases the powder magazine was located some distance from the installation to minimize the danger to the garrison from an accidental explosion. As the post grew, if indeed it did, with the addition of new units and a civilian population, new structures were erected by military personnel.

Congressional appropriations were scarce for fort construction, although civilian craftsmen were sometimes employed to build housing. This lack of funding caused the military to have to rely on their own people and to utilize whatever building materials were on hand. Given the circumstances, the soldiers sometimes managed to build quite suitable quarters for themselves and their officers. Other times their efforts were totally inadequate, and they merely succeeded in building a slum.

A typical fort was not enclosed by walls of any kind; the army relied instead on rapid movement and superior firepower as a defense against hostile Indians. Only on rare occasions was a fort assaulted, and it was usually more of a raid to steal horses and supplies than a concentrated attack. A scarcity of building materials also contributed to the lack of protective barriers. Most posts were built on the frontier, far

U.S. Army Period (1848-1861)

removed from the comforts of civilization, supplies, and materials, and had to be as self-sufficient as possible.

That the army succeeded in its mission to protect civilians and keep the Indians at bay was a testament to the rugged character of the officers and men who served in Texas.

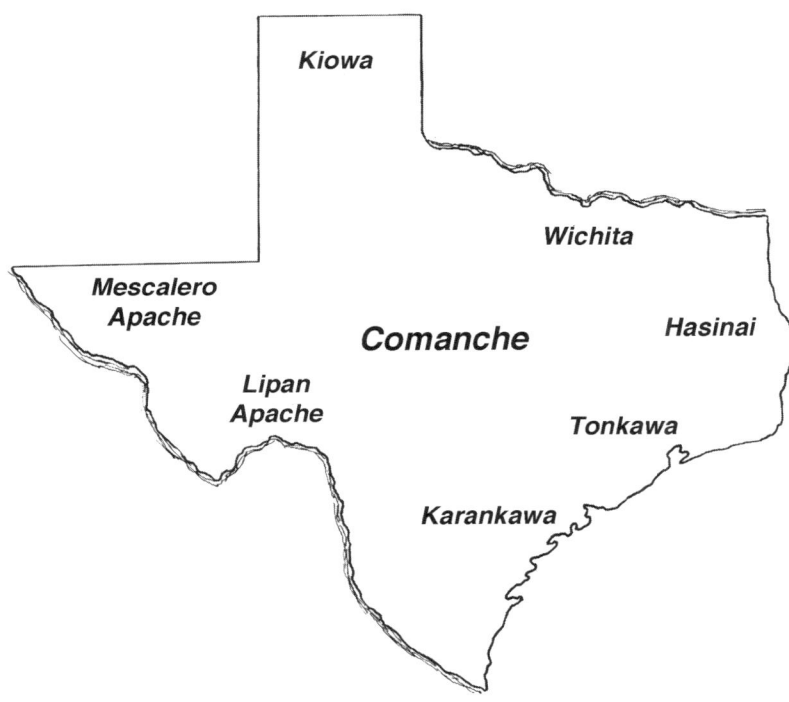

Between 1848 and 1900 the U.S. Army constructed nearly 150 forts and camps in the military department of Texas, the largest area of responsibility the army was charged with protecting and securing. Close to fifty sites became permanent forts while others seemed to disappear within a few short years of their establishment.

Fort Graham

Constructed on the site of an old Waco village in 1849 by units of the 2nd Dragoons, Fort Graham was abandoned in 1853. The original location of the fort is now at the bottom of a manmade lake, Lake Whitney, but much of the fort's construction material was relocated before the area was flooded. A reconstructed replica of a barracks building now occupies a site known as Fort Graham Park, 5.3 miles north of the town of Whitney.

Fort Lincoln

Established in 1849 as part of a line of posts that stretched from the Rio Grande to the Red River, the post was abandoned in 1852.

Fort Gates

Built on the military road between the town of Austin and Fort Graham in 1849 as a way station and outpost between those two major points, it was abandoned in 1852 when units of the 8th Infantry were withdrawn. The city of Gatesville derived its name from the fort, two years after the army departed.

Fort Merrill

Established by the 1st Infantry in 1850 in southern Texas to handle the troublesome area south of San Antonio and west of the Gulf of Mexico, it was abandoned in 1855.

Fort Terrett

Constructed in 1852, near the site of present-day town of Sonora, it was abandoned in 1854.

Camp Wood

Established on the ruins of a Spanish mission, San Lorenzo de la Santa Cruz, in the Texas Hill Country in 1857, the post was abandoned by Federal troops in 1861 and never reoccupied after the Civil War. Units of Texas Rangers used the post for several years in their ongoing war with Indians and Mexican bandits. The town of Camp Wood derives its name from the former installation.

Buffalo Springs

Lasting only five months, from July to November of 1867, the installation was abandoned in favor of the construction of Fort Richardson. Serving instead as a stagecoach stopover between Fort Richardson and Fort Sill (Oklahoma), the station actually occupied the site of a former Confederate outpost. The site was never officially named.

Camp Pena Colorado

Established in 1880 south of Forts Davis and Stockton at a fork in the Comanche War Trail that led into Mexico, it was raided a year after its opening not by Comanches but by Apaches. The outpost was abandoned in 1893.

Fort Ewell

Established on the south bank of the Nueces River near the Huajuico Crossing in 1852, the fort was situated in a poor location. The river frequently flooded the area around the fort, and there was no suitable timber available for construction. The adobe structures the soldiers erected lacked wooden braces and had to be roofed with canvas. Fresh food was so scarce that most of the garrison developed scurvy. The post was abandoned in 1854.

Fort Hancock

Originally established as Camp Rice in 1881, this was the last frontier fort built in Texas as a protection against Indians. It was located between Fort Bliss and Fort Quitman on the Mexican border, thirty miles northwest of Sierra Blanca. By the time the installation was renamed Fort Hancock in 1886, the Indian menace had all but vanished in the region. The

U.S. Army Period (1848-1861)

town of Fort Hancock, around the fort, experienced a dramatic drop in population, from two hundred to fifty residents, when the fort was abandoned in 1895.

In December of 1848, Camp Houston was established in the Texas Hill Country two miles southeast of the town of Fredericksburg. But the post was not there to protect the local settlers. They had already made a treaty with the local Comanches that both sides adhered to.

Fort Martin Scott

In 1849 Camp Houston was renamed Fort Martin Scott, and its garrison, alternating between a company of infantry and a company of cavalry, continued the duty of guarding the Fredericksburg-San Antonio road. The German settlers of the town had reached a peace agreement with the Comanche in 1847. The German delegates had been invited to a Comanche camp to work out terms, and when they approached the Indians' location they stopped their horses and fired their muskets into the air before proceeding. This gesture of peaceful intent, riding into the camp with discharged, unloaded weapons, so impressed the Comanche that they quickly reached terms with the Germans.

But friction between the Indians and new settlers and travelers was not covered in the treaty. Fort Martin Scott, located on Barons Creek, provided escort and protection for the outsiders moving into and through the fertile area. The soldiers also provided a source of cash for local merchants and were welcome in that capacity.

As the flow of settlers moved further west and the relative peace with the Comanche continued, the fort assumed the more mundane role of forage depot. In late 1853 the fort was abandoned, having served its purpose and now considered of no further use. During the Civil War the site was occupied by Confederate recruiters. From 1861 to 1865 the post served as

U.S. Army Period (1848-1861)

Fort Martin Scott barrack

a mustering station for enlistees on their way to the Confederate army and as a reminder to the local populace that they had voted overwhelmingly against secession. No Confederate troops were ever garrisoned there.

The U.S. Army briefly stationed troops at Fort Martin Scott in 1866, but when they were withdrawn that same year, the fort never served a military purpose again.

Later History

Fort Martin Scott Historic Site is now a park, leased from the town of Fredericksburg and maintained by the Fredericksburg Heritage Association. Only a few restored buildings remain at the site, located on Route 290. Costumed re-enactors provide tours and historical information on the Friday through Sunday hours of operation.

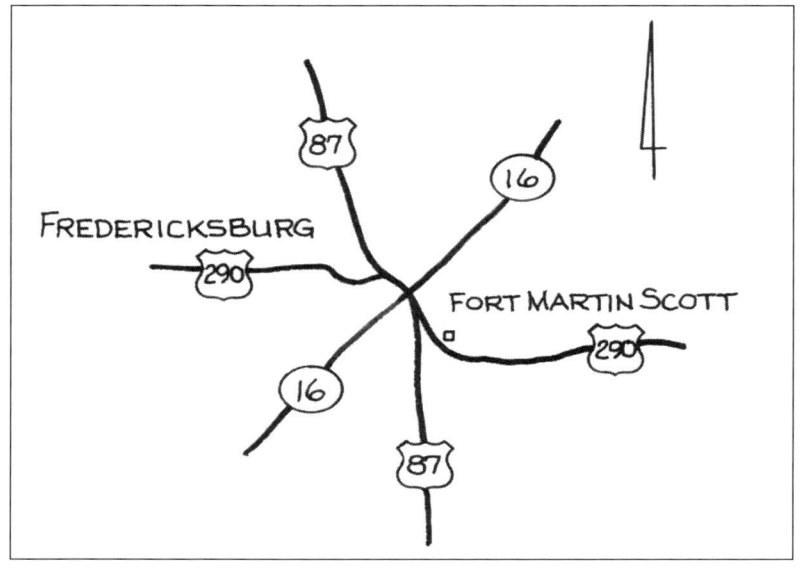

Fort Ringgold

Established after the Mexican War in 1848 as one of a series of forts along the Rio Grande, the installation was placed near the existing town of Rio Grande City. Known first as Camp Ringgold or Ringgold Barracks, the buildings erected by the garrison were flimsy and poorly constructed. The primary function of the soldiers was to guard the crossing, known as Davis Landing, between Texas and Mexico.

In 1861 the post fell into Confederate hands and was occupied until 1863, when Union forces retook the position. Strategically located on a route to Mexico over which Confederate cotton shipments were made, the area was hotly contested. In 1864 the fort was recaptured by the Confederates and used as a base of operations for attacks on Brownsville and the Union forces there. In 1865 the fort was

U.S. Army Period (1848-1861)

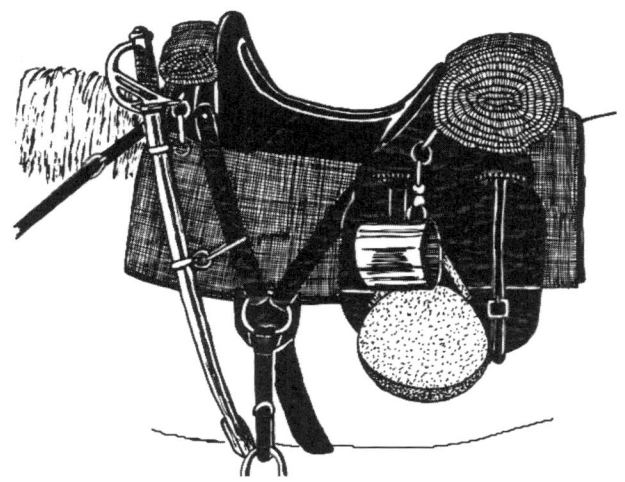

back under Federal control and a serious building program was undertaken.

By 1868 over 300 civilian construction laborers were working on site, doing a far better job than the soldiers ever could have. The wood frame and brick buildings being built would be the envy of every other fort in Texas. The enlisted men's barracks, for instance, were two-story company-sized structures that offered first-floor reading rooms, washrooms, and dining rooms. The second floors were open dormitory areas that slept an entire company of men without crowding. There were four such buildings erected at the fort. Officers quarters were one-and-a-half-story, eight-room structures that housed three officers each. In each forty-foot-by-fifty-four-foot building lived a captain, allotted four rooms, and two lieutenants, given two rooms apiece. In 1878 the post was officially named Fort Ringgold.

If Fort Quitman was considered the worst post in Texas for living conditions, Fort Ringgold was judged to be the best and most attractive. The parade ground was even lined with palm trees.

Later History

Fort Ringgold was closed down in 1906 and reopened in 1917 when internal conflicts in Mexico threatened to spill over into Texas. From 1917 until 1944 the fort continued to be occupied and was a much sought after duty assignment. In 1944 Fort Ringgold was deactivated and closed for good. In 1947 the remains at the fort cemetery were removed and reinterred at Fort Sam Houston National Cemetery in San Antonio. The fort site was sold to the Rio Grande Consolidated Independent School District in 1949.

Today the school district uses and maintains the buildings of Fort Ringgold in Rio Grande City. Two structures in particular continue to attract public interest, the post hospital and the Lee House. The Lee House was once occupied by Lt. Col. Robert E. Lee while he was on an inspection tour in 1860. When he was called back to Washington, Lee resigned his U.S. Army commission and became the most famous general of the Confederacy.

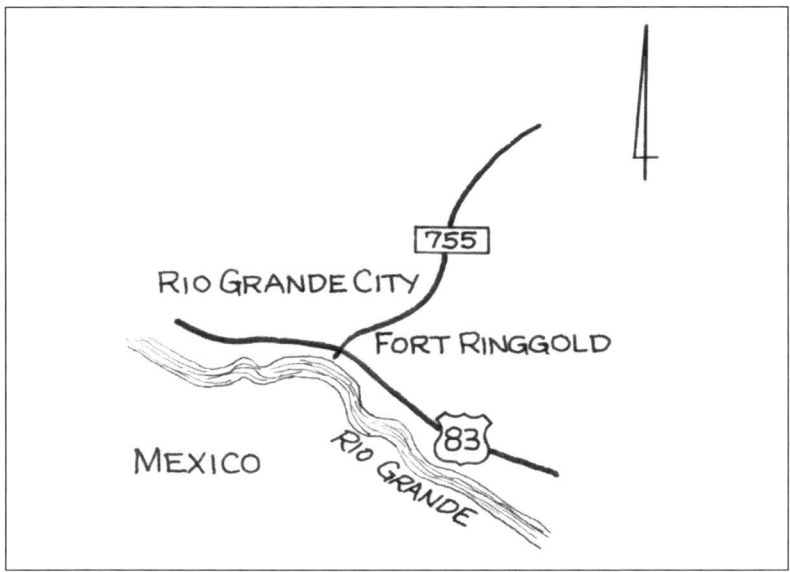

U.S. Army Period (1848-1861)

Fort Leaton

Fort Leaton was not a military post but a fortress-home and trading post built by Ben Leaton in 1848. Located on a terrace overlooking the Rio Grande, the massive home provided protection from attack by Apaches and Comanches for Leaton and his family, his employees, local settlers, and travelers.

More than forty rooms opened onto a large central courtyard inside the adobe enclosure whose walls averaged some fifteen feet in height. The rooms all had flat roofs that drained rainwater outside the walls with the use of mesquite gargolas, and each was floored with clay tiles. Each room had plastered and whitewashed walls and was fitted with doors and windows opening onto the courtyard. In the harsh West Texas environment, Fort Leaton was a place of safety and comfort.

Before his death in 1851, Ben Leaton cornered the market on trade with the local Indians and provided supplies for long-ranging army patrols. His widow and her new husband allowed units of the regular army and units of Texas Rangers to use their home as a base of operations on several occasions before selling it to John Burgess in 1861. Members of the Burgess family lived at Fort Leaton (it retained its name even under new ownership) until 1926. From 1927 to 1956 various rooms were lived in or used for storage.

Later History

Deeded to the state of Texas in 1967, along with almost twenty-five acres of land, Fort Leaton was designated a state historical park and opened to the public in 1978. Twenty-four of the forty rooms have been architecturally restored and reroofed. Facilities at the site include the historic ruins, the restored rooms, interpretive exhibits, and an audio-visual presentation. Fort Leaton also serves as the visitors center for Big Bend Ranch State Park, and a Texas state parks store is on site. The fort is open daily from 8 A.M. to 4:30 P.M. and is located four miles southeast of Presidio on FM 170. Admission is charged.

U.S. Army Period (1848-1861)

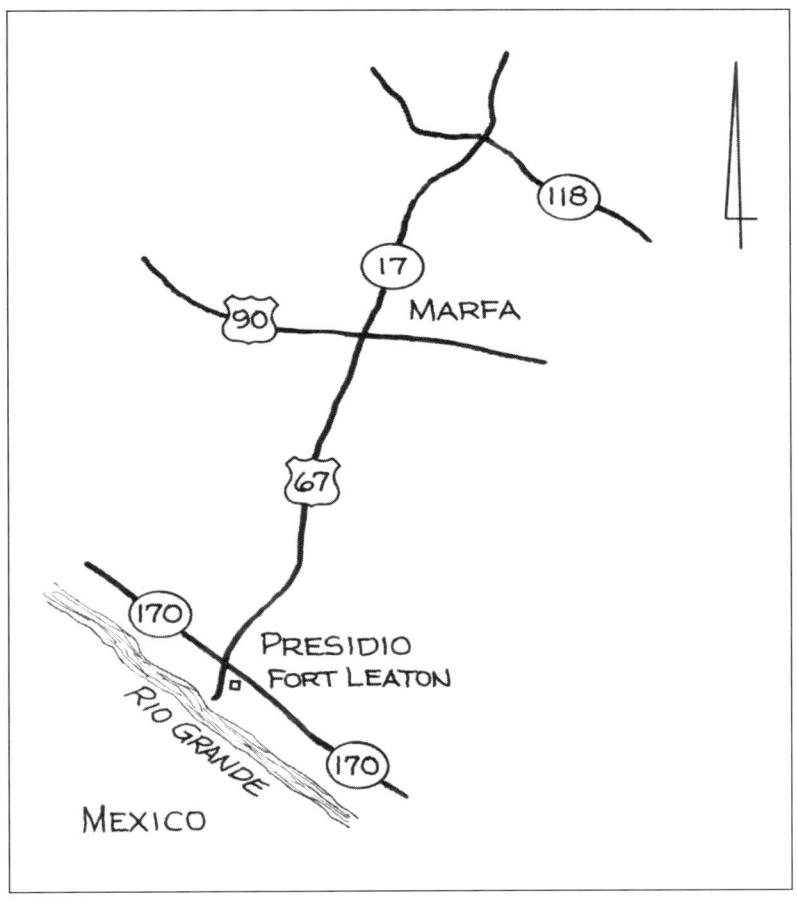

Established in 1848, the military post at El Paso was considered permanent only to the area. The actual site was moved up to six times in order to effectively combat Indian raids and maintain American control over territory won in the war with Mexico. This westernmost fort in the republic, and later state, of Texas has been held by Federal troops longer than any other fort in the area.

Fort Bliss

In its first years of existence Fort Bliss occupied several sites, including Smith's Ranch, Stephenson's (or Concordia) Ranch, Magoffinsville, and Hart's Mill. It was at Hart's Mill that the U.S. government actually purchased the land, instead of leasing it, in 1878. Throughout its tenure at the Hart's Mill site, work went slowly on the construction of permanent buildings to house the garrison because of frequent campaigns against hostile Apaches. The Victorio uprising of 1879 and the Geronimo campaign of 1885-86 drew away much-needed laborers. The Congress had refused to allocate funds for the fort's construction, so the soldiers stationed there were engaged in building their own quarters. Any construction activity would all but cease each time the garrison took the field. Earlier sites of Fort Bliss had fared no better.

In 1861 Confederate forces had taken over the fort for use as headquarters for their operations in the Southwest during the Civil War. It was from here that campaigns into Arizona and New Mexico were launched. Located at Magoffinsville at the time, the fort was destroyed in 1862 in the face of advancing Union troops. When the Federals reoccupied the ruins of their fort, they discovered the retreating Confederates had

U.S. Army Period (1848-1861)

left behind their sick and wounded and all the fort's medical supplies for their care in captivity.

Conditions at the fort were less than ideal for the Union troops. Almost no structures or equipment remained for their use, and the war in the East sapped any resources that could have been used to reestablish the post. In 1868 the garrison was moved to the site of the Concordia Ranch, where two barracks and several adobe buildings were built. Yet, despite the rough shelter at hand, the new location tested the mettle of the hardiest of souls. For ten years the post hung on, like a tick on a starving dog, as the rigors of battling the hostile desert elements and even more fierce Apaches pounded the garrison down. Finally, in 1876, the fort was abandoned. In 1878 the Army returned and bought 135 acres of land at Hart's Mill.

From 1878 to 1893, Fort Bliss provided the necessary protection in the region that permitted the town of El Paso, and to a large extent the Mexican town of Juarez across the Rio Grande, to grow and prosper. This was because Fort Bliss was strategically located at a pass through the mountains along the Rio Grande between the United States and Mexico. The control of movement of undesirable elements and mobility provided to the troops proved no match, however, to the powerful railroad lobby.

The site of Fort Bliss was a much-desired location by the Southern Pacific Railroad. By exerting strong influence on the U.S. Congress and Texas Legislature, the railroad was able to obtain a right-of-way through the fort. With the military powerless to stop them, the Southern Pacific and the Santa Fe railroads actually laid tracks right through the Fort Bliss parade ground. In 1893 the Army finally surrendered and moved Fort Bliss, for the last time, to an area fives miles northeast of El Paso.

Later History

Today Fort Bliss is a U.S. Army Air Defense Center and Combat Training Center for foreign, allied countries. The remains of one previous fort location can be found at the 1800 block of Doniphan Street in the city of El Paso.

Four structures exist there, two officers quarters buildings and two enlisted mans barracks. The officers quarters are two-story structures and somewhat ornate in the Victorian style of architectural detailing. Each entrance doorway has single doors with sidelights beside and a transom above. The upper story windows are accented by low gables. Originally a veranda porch ran the entire length of each building front, providing shade for the first floor living quarters. It was later cut down to smaller length.

Not untypically, the barracks are plain structures of adobe. The buildings are long and the facades plainly adorned with alternating windows and doors, one window and door per interior barrack room. Since the comfort, what could be provided, of the officers and their families was of more concern than the comfort of the enlisted men, it is not surprising that the former officers quarters are today used as apartments.

The Fort Bliss Museum stands now on the site of the former Magoffinsville location once held by both Federal and Confederate troops. A replica of the original adobe fort has been constructed and presents displays from the Texas frontier era. Located near the intersection of Pershing and Pleasanton Roads, the museum is open daily from 9 A.M. to 4:30 P.M. except on Christmas, New Year's, Easter, and Thanksgiving.

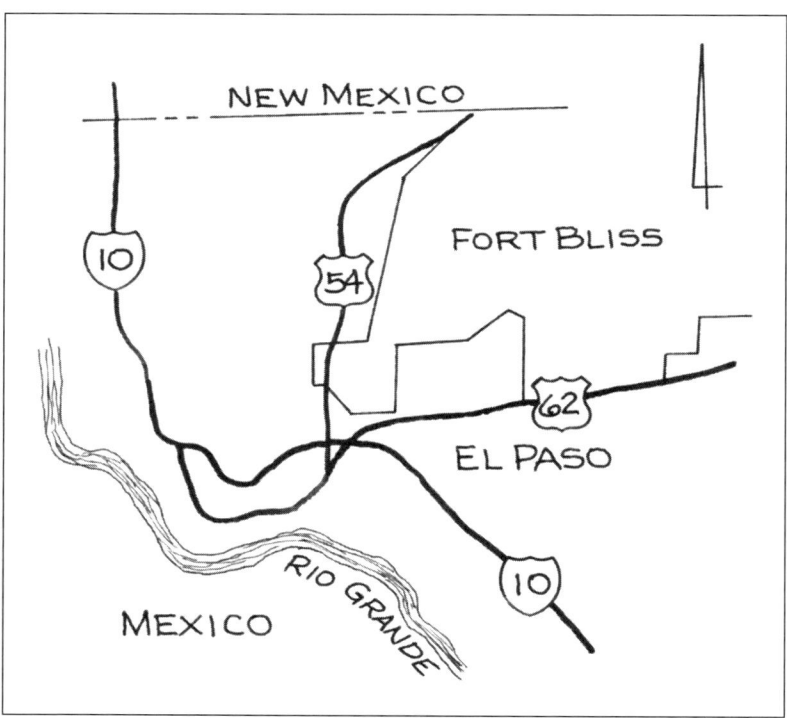

U.S. Army Period (1848-1861)

Some forts came and went so quickly that only a few temporary shelters marked their passing. One such fort left behind a community that would eventually grow into the twenty-eighth largest city in the United States.

Fort Worth

Units of Company F of the 2nd Dragoons established Camp Worth in June of 1849 on a high hill overlooking the Trinity River. That same year the name was changed to Fort Worth, but no permanent structures were ever built there. A few ramshackle wooden barracks were erected, but the troops still baked in the summer and froze in the winter, exposed as they were on a barren hill. As no real Indian threat ever presented itself, the soldiers spent much of their time in the small towns

of Fort Worth and Dallas. In fact, the only Indian encounter recorded at Fort Worth was when a band of Taovaya warriors were sent running by a single shot from the fort's only cannon.

In 1851 two companies of the 8th Infantry replaced the dragoons, or cavalry, at Fort Worth. By 1853 these troops were reassigned to Fort Belknap, and the hilltop site was abandoned. Local Fort Worth merchants immediately took over the barracks buildings for use as stores.

No trace of the military installation of Fort Worth exists today.

Fort Croghan

Originally the site of a Texas Ranger campsite on Hamilton Creek known as McCulloch's Station, the fort was established in 1849. After displacing the rangers, it was decided to move the fort across the river and three miles upstream. The fort was known as Camp Croghan, then Camp Hamilton, and finally Fort Croghan.

The buildings of the fort were sturdy and comfortable, of oak construction and covered with shingles. But no sooner had the structures been completed than the troops began to be transferred to other posts. The exodus began in 1853, and the fort was finally abandoned in 1855. Civilians moved into the buildings after the last troops left.

Later History

By 1940 only stone foundations remained to indicate the site of Fort Croghan; the last surviving structure had been torn down in 1922. In the early 1960s the Burnet County

U.S. Army Period (1848-1861)

Historical Society undertook to rebuild Fort Croghan without actually reconstructing it. Acquiring several old historic buildings in the area that had been built around the same time as the fort, the Society simply moved the structures to the site and called it Fort Croghan. By 1967 three buildings had been restored and furnished with authentic pieces of furniture.

Today the Fort Croghan Museum consists of a stone powder magazine and several log and stone buildings, all accurate to the time period. Exhibits include old weapons, furniture, and carriages. The museum is open from April through August, Thursday through Saturday from 10 A.M. to 5 P.M. and is located on Highway 29 West in Burnet.

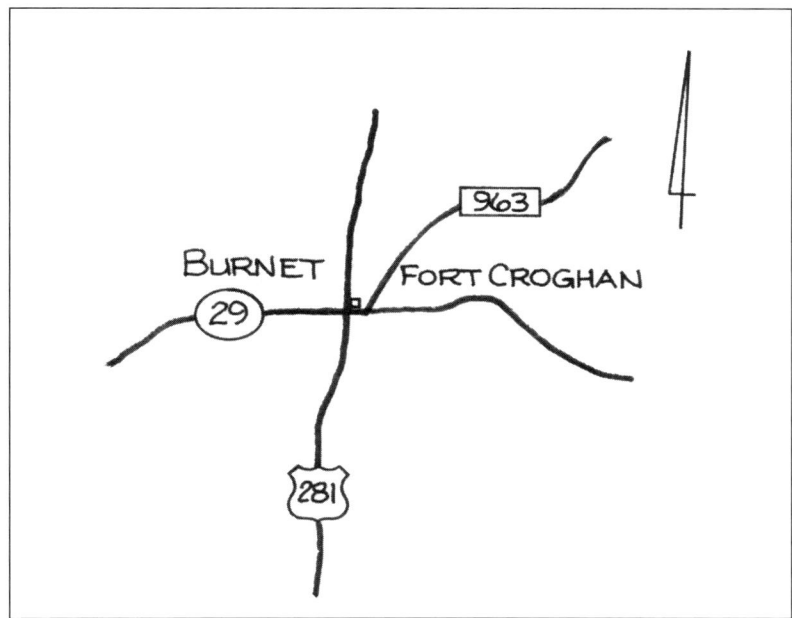

Fort Duncan

Established in 1849 on the east bank of the lower Rio Grande, Fort Duncan was garrisoned by three companies of the 1st Infantry to protect the area from Indians. The first structures were of wood construction, totally inadequate as living quarters but more suited for temporary shelters. This was due, in large part, to the fact that the land the fort occupied had been neither leased nor purchased by the government, and if the site was to be later moved, no real work would be done at this one. In 1853 the property owner, a San Antonio resident, leased the land to the Army for fifteen years, and more permanent stone buildings were soon under construction.

Local stone was used, piled together rather than shaped and fitted. A company of artillerymen assigned to Fort Duncan even chipped in eighty dollars of their own money to

U.S. Army Period (1848-1861)

help pay the labor and equipment costs of hauling the stones to the building site. The soldiers, though, built the structures themselves. The resulting buildings were devoid of any architectural detailing, and large stones were placed at the corners of the buildings to keep the walls from collapsing. Wood was used for roofing and framing in doors and windows.

By 1856 the building project had been completed, most of the officers quarters having been paid for by the officers themselves, without any hope of a government reimbursement. In May of 1859 the post was temporarily abandoned but was regarrisoned in March of 1860 when Mexican bandit activity increased in the area. The Eagle Pass crossing of the Rio Grande nearby made movement in and out of Mexico easy for the bandits, and American settlements along the border were inviting targets.

When the Confederacy occupied the fort during the Civil War, it became known as the Rio Grande Station. Through this point flowed munitions and supplies from Mexico, in return for cotton, destined for the Texas Confederate troops. When the Confederates set up a series of camps from the Red River to the Rio Grande, outposts a day's ride apart, Camp Rabb was situated only a short distance from Fort Duncan/Rio Grande Station. The two sites were often mentioned together as if they were one installation.

Federal troops returned to Fort Duncan in 1868, and in 1870 the Seminole-Negro Indian scouts were organized at the fort before being sent to Fort Clark to serve. The fort was garrisoned by Federal troops until 1890, when units of the Texas National Guard assumed the duties there. Internal disturbances in Mexico caused the return of the regular army in 1917 to guard the border crossing at Eagle Pass. Fort Duncan was permanently abandoned in 1922.

Later History

The city of Eagle Pass purchased the site of Fort Duncan for use as a recreational park in 1938. Repair and restoration was undertaken on the whitewashed stone buildings. A restored infantry barracks once served as a country club and, during World War II, an officers club for an Army Air Force flying school nearby. The Fort Duncan Museum is housed in the former post headquarters building, and its exhibits include photographs and artifacts dating from the early history of the region to the twentieth century.

The museum is open Monday through Saturday from 1 P.M. to 5 P.M. and donations are accepted. Fort Duncan Park is located between Monroe and Garrison Streets in Eagle Pass.

U.S. Army Period (1848-1861)

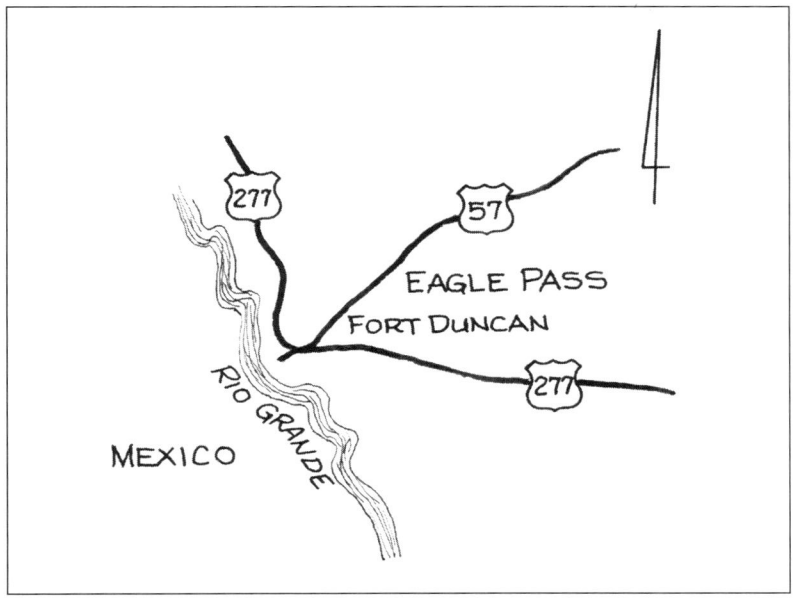

Fort McIntosh

Constructed on a bluff overlooking the Rio Grande west of the town of Laredo by troops sent from Fort Ringgold in 1849, Fort McIntosh was one of a series of forts along the newly created border with Mexico in the aftermath of the Mexican War. The fort itself, built in 1853, was a star-shaped earthen enclosure that measured 100 feet by 100 feet. The powder magazine was a stone vault buried inside the southeast part of the fort, accessed by steps down and secured with iron doors. Each point of the star was a raised cannon platform, providing complete command of the area surrounding the fort. Throughout the early occupation of the site and construction of the fort, the troops lived in tents. Upon completion of the earthen enclosure, work was begun on permanent housing for the garrison.

In the next five years the installation built up in the vicinity of the fort would come to include thirty buildings arranged around a central parade ground. The garrison, always on patrol and campaign against Lipan Apache and Comanche raiders, would grow to over 400 men. In 1858 the majority of the garrison was reassigned to Florida, leaving only twenty-six men to man the fort. The remaining men were withdrawn in 1859, and Fort McIntosh stood abandoned.

The town of Laredo immediately claimed the site and auctioned off all the buildings to private citizens. But Mexican bandit activity in the region had begun to increase, and in 1860 two companies of infantry returned to the fort. Just over a year later the garrison would become prisoners of war when Confederate forces, comprised mostly of newly recruited citizens of Laredo under the leadership of former mayor Santos Benavides, took over the installation.

The Confederates at Fort McIntosh helped protect shipments of cotton into Mexico during the Civil War. Since the Union blockade had closed off import and export from the Southern coastal ports, supplies and material were channeled overland to and from Mexico and its ports. Late in the war Union forces marched upriver along the Rio Grande and attacked Fort McIntosh. The fort successfully repulsed several assaults, and the Federals withdrew back to the coast. At war's end, though, the fort was reoccupied by a company of the 62nd Infantry, black soldiers newly enlisted in the army of the United States.

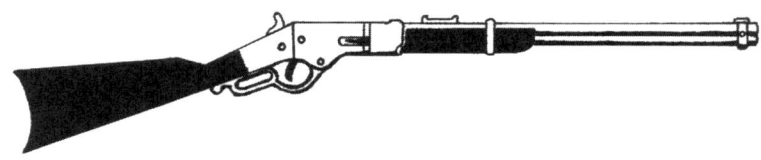

U.S. Army Period (1848-1861)

From 1865 until 1880 the infantrymen were quartered in tents. In 1868 a hospital, guardhouse, and a few adobe buildings for the officers were constructed, but the real building activity at Fort McIntosh would not start until 1877. From that year onward the size of the fort would grow rapidly. In 1880 several barracks were built, in 1886 a new hospital and guardhouse, in 1887 a granary, and in 1890 new quarters for officers and noncommissioned officers, a bathhouse, boiler house, pump house, and commissary. The telegraph came to Fort McIntosh in 1878 and the railroad in 1881.

The years between the Spanish-American War and World War I, 1898 to 1917, were very active at Fort McIntosh. The years 1910 through 1917 saw troops from the fort camped all along the border to prevent entry by Mexican revolutionaries during that country's political upheaval. Many units stationed at the fort during that period would later see service in World War I—the 23rd and 26th Infantry and the 14th Cavalry. Between World War I and World War II the fort was headquarters to the 8th Service Command and home for the Civil Air Patrol. In 1947 Fort McIntosh was closed in favor of the nearby Laredo Air Force Base.

Later History

Most of the buildings and land of Fort McIntosh were turned over to Laredo Junior College for use as a campus in 1947. A sandstone wall now encloses the remains of the original star-shaped fort, overgrown with vegetation and partially collapsed from years of abandonment and neglect, its outline still barely visible. The old chapel, the guardhouse, a warehouse, and the commissary remain in use by the college. The Fort McIntosh site is located on Washington Street on the banks of the Rio Grande in the city of Laredo.

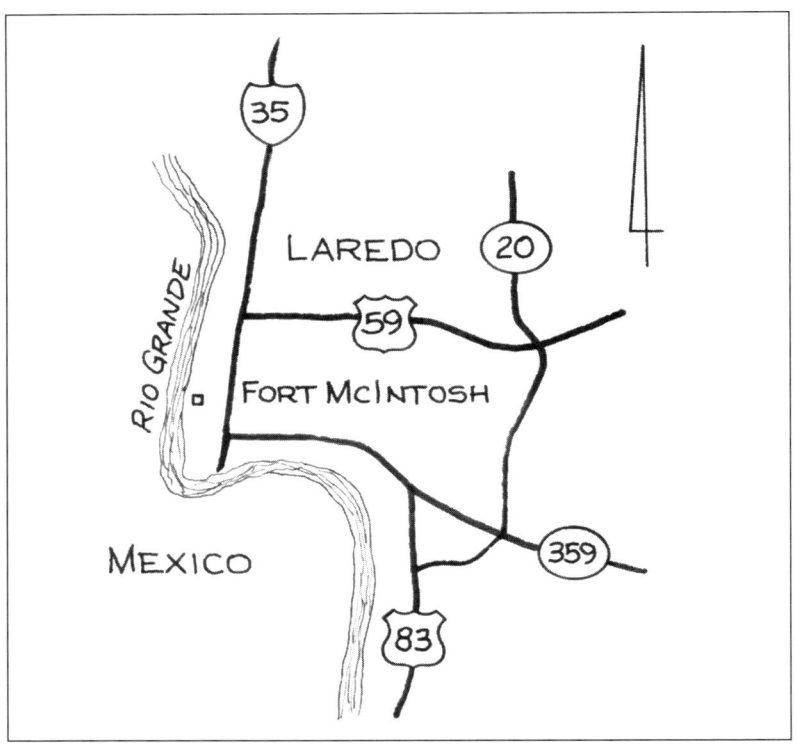

U.S. Army Period (1848-1861)

Fort Inge

Established in early 1849 as one of a series of post-Mexican War installations charged with guarding the border, the fort, originally called Camp Leona, was built on the east bank of the Leona River four miles above Woll's Crossing. The post was renamed Fort Inge later in the year. Of the dozen or so buildings erected around a central parade ground, only one, the post hospital, was constructed of cut limestone. The rest of the structures were made of upright logs plastered with mud and then whitewashed.

Fort Inge was situated near a major turnoff point on the road from San Antonio to El Paso. The turnoff went to Eagle Pass, location of Fort Duncan, and crossed the Rio Grande into Mexico. The rich abundance of water, wood, and favorable soil soon drew farmers to the vicinity of the fort, and the town of Encina began there around 1855, being renamed Uvalde in 1856. The garrison of Fort Inge guarded the settlement against Indian raids, provided escorts for supply wagon trains, and offered protection for all from Mexican bandits.

When occupied by Confederate forces in 1861, the fort became a vital point in protecting shipments of cotton to Mexico through Eagle Pass. The outpost of Camp Dix was only seven miles away from the fort. Dix, established in 1862 as part of a line of outposts a day's ride apart from the Red River to the Rio Grande, became closely identified with Fort Inge. Sometime during the Confederate occupation of the fort, a low wall of stacked stones was put up around the site, enclosing it.

Federal troops returned to Fort Inge in 1866 and remained until 1869 when the garrison was transferred to Fort McKavett. In 1871 Fort Inge was effectively deconstructed by troops sent to gather timber and stones for the building of

Fort Clark. The site of Fort Inge was used as a Texas Ranger campsite until 1884.

Fort Inge County Park now exists where the fort once stood. It is located on FM 140, a mile and a half south of Uvalde.

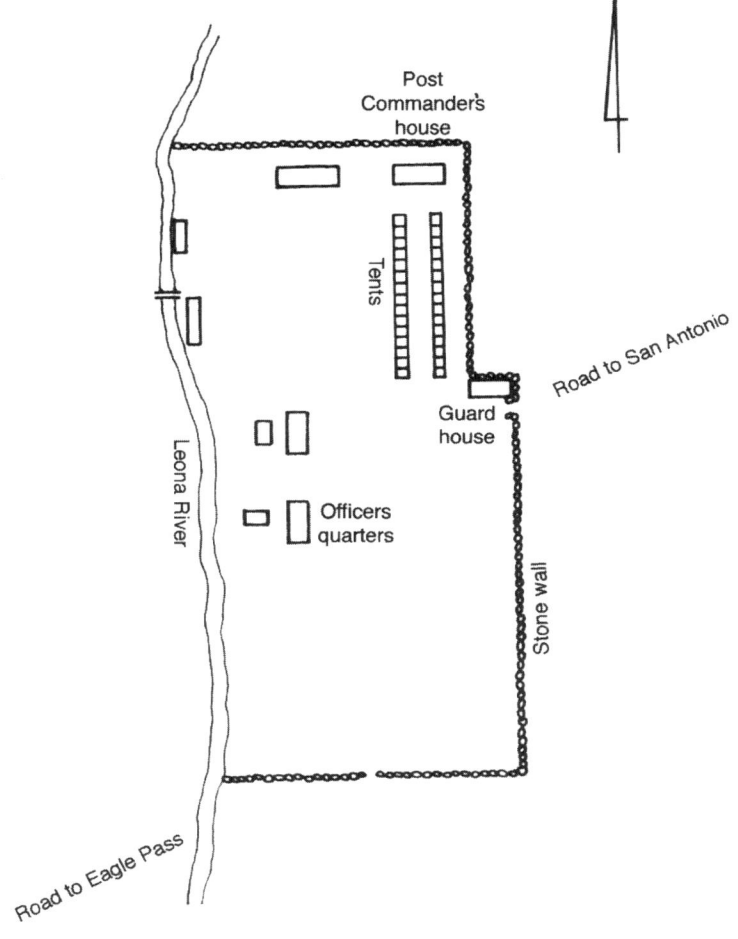

Fort Inge 1868

U.S. Army Period (1848-1861)

In the 1850s one fifth of the U.S. Army served in Texas. Aided by state troops and Texas Rangers, the soldiers sought to curb and eliminate raids on white settlements by Indian warriors.

Fort Belknap

Established in June of 1851 ten miles from the confluence of Clear Fork and the Brazos River, the site was chosen by Brevet Brigadier General William G. Belknap, and the fort was named after him. The first buildings were of log construction and consisted of a commissary and living quarters.

Fort Belknap was the northern anchor of a string of forts stretching southwest to the Rio Grande. In the years following its establishment, the wooden buildings were gradually replaced by sturdy sandstone structures. These would come to include a new commissary, a bakery, quarters for six companies of infantry, a powder magazine, officers quarters, and a hospital. Also built were stables and a sawmill. Life at Fort Belknap was anything but easy, situated deep in Kiowa and Comanche territory as it was. Troops from the fort were in almost constant conflict with the local tribes even though the garrison was understaffed and unable to provide adequate protection in the region. But despite the warfare in the area, Fort Belknap served as an important station on the Butterfield Overland stage route between 1858 and 1861.

U.S. Army Period (1848-1861)

In October of 1858 soldiers from Fort Belknap struck a decisive blow against the Comanche. Four companies of the 2nd Cavalry completed a forced march of ninety miles in thirty-six hours and fell upon the sleeping Comanche village of Chief Buffalo Hump at Rush Spring. The battle was fought in the early morning fog, making concentrated troop movements next to impossible, so the troopers charged into the village, and a bloody riot ensued. After an hour and a half of savage fighting, much of it hand-to-hand, the Comanches fled. Fifty-six warriors and two women lay dead, one hundred twenty lodges were in flames, and three hundred horses were rounded up. The troopers suffered three dead, thirteen wounded, and one missing.

At the beginning of the Civil War, Fort Belknap was abandoned by Federal troops and taken over by forces of the Texas Frontier Regiment of the Confederate Army. The fort was used throughout the war as a striking point against Kiowa and Comanche raiders. The Confederates had even less luck controlling the area than the Federals had.

Returning to the fort after the Civil War, Federal troops soon discovered the water supply becoming unreliable. In September of 1867 the fort was officially abandoned, but in years following this action small units of troops were stationed there. By 1875 Fort Belknap stood in ruins.

Later History

In 1936 some of the original buildings of Fort Belknap were restored or rebuilt by concerned local citizens. The only original structure to survive after the fort's abandonment was the powder magazine. Rebuilt structures included the two-story commissary and five barracks. A museum and archive are operated at the site by the Fort Belknap Society in the commissary and one barrack.

The Commissary Museum features various artifacts from the period of occupation. Tools, furniture, weapons, and an impressive collection of arrowheads are on display. Also to be viewed are many photographs of former officers stationed at Fort Belknap.

The Fort Belknap archives are housed in a restored barracks and include documents and military records of the fort's history.

Fort Belknap Park is located three miles south of Newcastle on State Highway 251. It is open daily, except Wednesday, from 9 A.M. to 5 P.M.

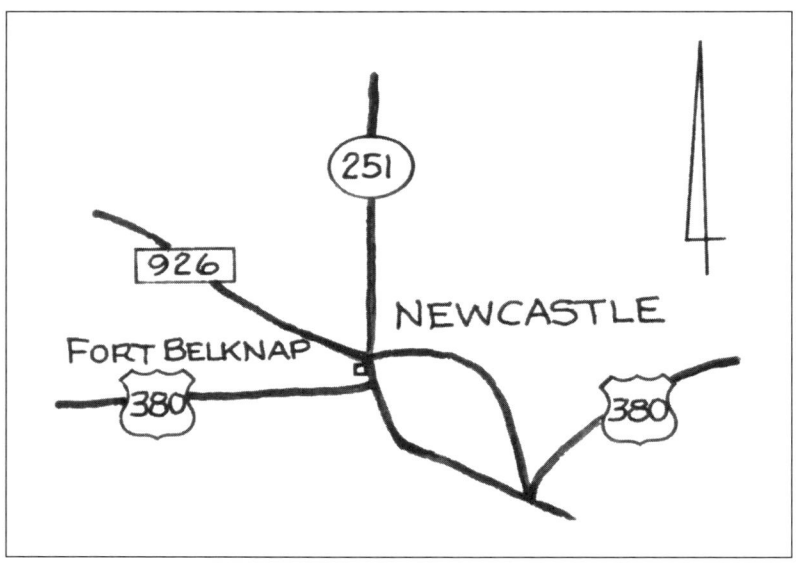

U.S. Army Period (1848-1861)

Although never officially named, this fort was known by a colorful title that derived from either one of two phenomenon, perhaps both. The hill upon which the fort was built seemed, at a distance, to rise dramatically up from the plains surrounding it; but as it was approached, it appeared to shrink in height and to level out. There was also the tale of a ghostly Indian warrior seen wandering the area on moonlit nights.

Fort Phantom Hill

Established on the Clear Fork of the Brazos River near its junction with Elm Creek in 1851, the fort seemed cursed with hardship from the start. To begin with, the commander of the detachment assigned the duty of constructing the post, five companies of the 5th Infantry, was unfamiliar with the area and picked a site other than where he had been told to put the fort.

The water supply was unreliable; Elm Creek often dried up, and the Clear Fork ran slow and brackish. An eighty-foot well also ran dry frequently. Water had to be hauled in by wagon, the barrels being filled at a spring four miles upriver from the fort. Stone was in abundance, but timber had to be brought in from as far as forty miles away. Despite the scarcity of handy materials and the harsh living conditions, the troops dutifully labored at constructing suitable quarters for themselves.

The commissary, guardhouse, and powder magazine were built entirely of stone; the hospital and officers quarters were made of oak logs on stone foundations. The enlisted men lived in timber post huts, upright logs plastered with mud and covered with thatched roofs. All the buildings had stone chimneys.

If there was one bright spot in the occupation of Fort Phantom Hill, it was that the local Indians—Wichitas, Kickapoos, Kiowas, and Comanches—seemed friendly and willing to tolerate the fort's presence. Mounted warriors could have easily overwhelmed foot soldiers in such an isolated position, but when the fort was visited, it was for peaceful trading. This lack of hostility led to the abandonment of the fort in 1854.

Shortly after the troops departed, every wooden building in the fort was set ablaze and burned to the ground by a person, or persons, unknown.

In 1858 the stone structures were repaired and used as a station by the Butterfield Overland Mail stage line. In 1861 the station was occupied by Confederate cavalry of the 1st Regiment Texas Mounted Rifles and remained in their hands until 1862. The site was used after that by long-ranging patrols and Texas Ranger units as a temporary campsite.

Fort Phantom Hill served briefly as a subpost of Fort Griffin and was lightly garrisoned for that purpose in 1871. The small town that had established itself near the post was a major shipping post for buffalo hides by 1876. By 1881, when the buffalo were gone and the Indians subdued, both the fort and the town had long since been abandoned.

Later History

Today Fort Phantom Hill stands in ghostly ruin, as befits its name, overgrown with prairie weeds and cactus. Three stone buildings remain—the commissary, guardhouse, and powder magazine—and are maintained. Over a dozen chimneys stand above the remains of stone foundations like silent limestone sentinels. Throughout the site, open daily, a series of interpretive signs point out important details and history. Fort

U.S. Army Period (1848-1861)

Phantom Hill is located north of Abilene, off of Interstate 20 on FM 600.

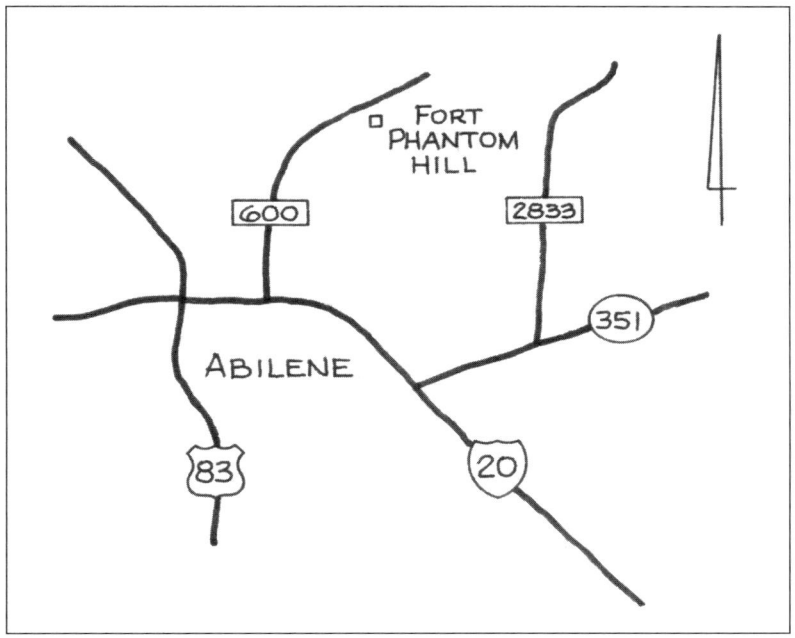

Fort Mason

Established in 1851 at a site known as Post Oak Hill near Comanche and Centennial Creeks, Fort Mason carried on an aggressive campaign against Kiowa, Lipan Apache, and Comanche to drive them from the region. So successful was this military intervention that the post was closed several times throughout its history as trouble with the Indians ebbed and flowed. The fort was first closed in 1854 and reopened in 1856.

In 1861 the post was occupied by Confederate forces, who kept 200 Union sympathizers incarcerated there. By 1862 the Confederates had moved out; their defensive lines were drawn closer together in Texas because of a manpower shortage. Camp Llano, one of a series of camps a day's ride apart, was situated nine miles east of Fort Mason and tried to take up the slack created when the fort was abandoned. The fort was reoccupied by Federal troops in 1866.

By then most of the twenty-five stone buildings were in sore need of repair. The barracks, officers quarters, guardhouse, hospital, storehouses, and stables were practically uninhabitable, but little effort was put into reconstruction. The desertion rate at Fort Mason soared, as did the number of court-martials, and in early 1869 the fort was ordered closed. In 1870 several companies of Texas Rangers took over the fort and tried to make some repairs to the buildings. But by 1871 the ranger units had either been reassigned or discharged, and Fort Mason was abandoned for the last time. The stones from the crumbling buildings were carted away by local civilians for use in constructing their homes. Many houses in the nearby town of Mason began with building materials from the fort.

U.S. Army Period (1848-1861)

Later History

In 1975 a group of local citizens began to rebuild one of the stone officers quarters at Fort Mason. Using original stones still scattered around the site, the building was erected on one of the few remaining stone foundations. The reconstructed officers quarters is located on the crest of Post Hill, five blocks south of the Mason courthouse. It is owned by the Mason County Historical Society.

The Mason County Museum is housed in the old town schoolhouse that was made entirely from stones taken from Fort Mason in the 1870s. The museum is open daily from 8 to 3 and is located on Moody Street in Mason.

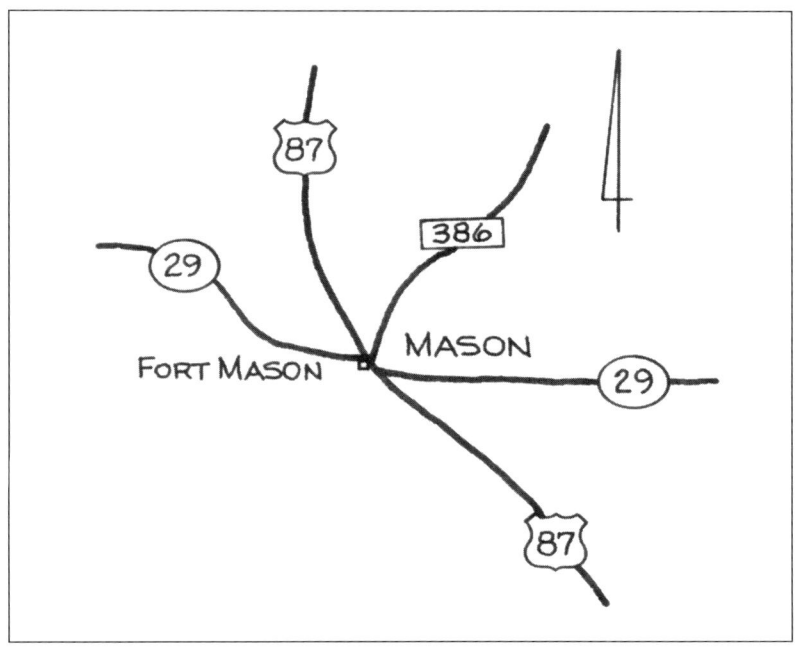

A strategic installation along the El Paso-San Antonio Road, the post charged with protection of frontier settlements and control of the Mexican border was also home for a special unit of the army, the Seminole-Negro Indian scouts.

Fort Clark

Established in 1852 at Las Moras Creek, Fort Clark would serve with distinction for nearly one hundred years from one century into the next. In that extended time almost every cavalry regiment in the U.S. Army would be stationed there at one time or another, as well as many infantry and artillery regiments.

Initially, Fort Clark was a quite uncomfortable duty assignment. Log buildings were poorly constructed of green wood, which shrank as it dried and provided convenient gaps for all manner of varmits to enter uninvited. A morning ritual at the fort was to expel insect and animal intruders from the living quarters. Additionally, clothing issued the troops was too warm for the environment of West Texas. In winter, though, when the clothes were well suited, the buildings were largely cold and unheated. In 1856 fireplaces and chimneys were added. Despite the hardships, the soldiers performed their duties with spirit. The road was guarded, wagons and settlers were escorted safely through the area, and the border with Mexico was patrolled against raids from Indians and Mexican bandits.

Federal troops were withdrawn from Fort Clark in 1861 and Confederate troops occupied the post. The new garrison, aided by companies of Texas Rangers, tried to carry on the work of their Union predecessors with varying degrees of success. But emboldened Comanches raided the area in ever

U.S. Army Period (1848-1861)

increasing numbers. At the conclusion of the Civil War, Fort Clark, an important outpost, was immediately reoccupied by the Federals with units of the newly formed black regiments, the 10th Cavalry and 24th and 25th Infantry.

In the 1870s construction of native limestone buildings was undertaken. At the same time, increased campaigns against the Indians were mounted. In 1872 the recruiting of Seminole-Negro Indian scouts to serve at Fort Clark allowed the U.S. Cavalry to pursue hostiles into northern Mexico.

The scouts, descendants of Seminole Indians and escaped slaves, had lived in the region since their people had settled it in the 1840s. They had served with the Mexican army in Coahuila from 1850 to 1870, their scouting abilities and knowledge of the terrain greatly enhancing the ability of the army to protect that northern province of Mexico. Lured away from the Mexicans in 1872, the Seminole-Negro Indian scouts

would perform stellar service for the United States at Fort Clark until they were disbanded in 1914.

In 1873 U.S. troops struck across the Rio Grande into Mexico. Villages of Kickapoo and Mescalero and Lipan Apaches were burned. Heated objections to this armed invasion of their country by the Mexican government failed to halt the army's pursuit of hostiles to their Mexican strongholds. In 1877 and 1878, units of the U.S. Cavalry actually encountered elements of the Mexican army while trespassing in that country on their search-and-destroy missions. Cool-headed field commanders on both sides avoided direct conflict, and war between the United States and Mexico was averted. In 1880 orders from Washington officially halted the practice of pursuing Indians and bandits into Mexico.

After the frontier was settled and peace came to the region, Fort Clark continued to serve as a horse cavalry training post. Its now comfortable buildings and location near a natural spring that kept the countryside well watered and lush made an assignment to the post a sought-after goal. Many a soldier considered garrison duty at Fort Clark a reward for outstanding military service.

During World War II, Fort Clark served as a German P.O.W. camp. The U.S. Army deactivated the fort in 1946.

Later History

Fort Clark today is probably the most well preserved of the original Texas forts not open to the public as such, but as a private recreational community. After its closure it was purchased and used as a guest ranch until a private corporation acquired it in 1971. More than forty of the original structures are listed in the National Register of Historic Places and now serve in a wide variety of uses. Stone barracks built

U.S. Army Period (1848-1861)

in 1872 are now utilized as motel rooms, and the guardhouse has been turned into a museum, named appropriately The Old Guardhouse Jail Cavalry Museum. A restaurant and lounge occupy the former post officers club.

The nearby Seminole Indian cemetery contains the graves of four members of that scout unit who were awarded the Medal of Honor during their service to the United States Cavalry in the 1870s Indian Wars.

The museum, focal point of the 2,700-acre gated resort now known as Fort Clark Springs, features exhibits of the history of the post and many of the famous military men who served there. Most notable of the officers who went on to future fame are General Jonathan M. Wainwright and General George S. Patton Jr. The museum is open Saturday and Sunday from 1 P.M. to 4 P.M. and is operated by the Fort Clark Historical Society.

Fort Clark Springs is located on U.S. 90, 120 miles west of San Antonio and 31 miles east of Del Rio on the Mexican border.

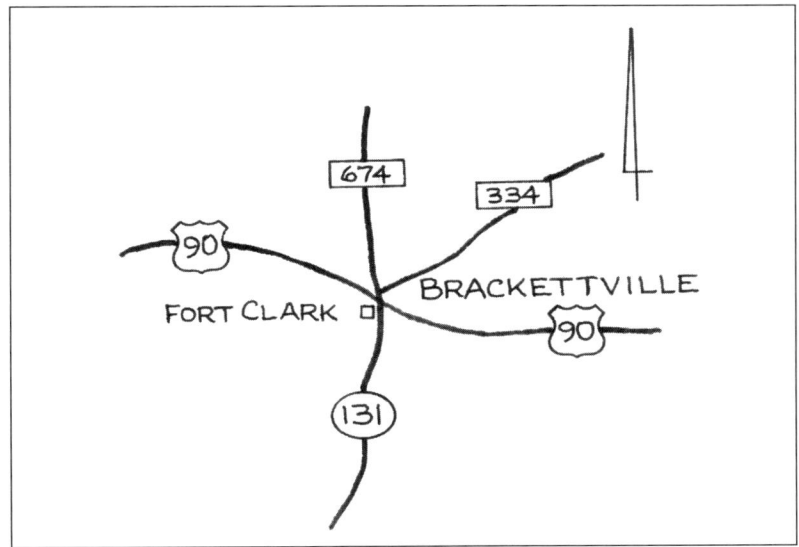

Fort Chadbourne

Established in 1852 by two companies of the 8th Infantry to combat Indian activity in the area of Oak Creek, the fort served as a way station on the Butterfield Overland stage route from 1858 to 1861.

Confederate forces occupied the fort in 1861, after Federal troops were withdrawn, and continued the aggressive campaign to keep the Indians in check the Union soldiers had been engaged in. Members of the 1st Regiment of Texas Mounted Rifles and units of Texas Rangers garrisoned the fort until they were ordered to leave in 1862, but they continued to use the site intermittently until the end of the war. In late 1864 Confederate forces were mustered at the fort to mount a major expedition against the Indian tribes moving through the region. At Dove Creek, in January of 1865, over 300 Confederates attacked a Kickapoo village. Unfortunately for the attackers, the Kickapoos, over 700 strong, had been armed by Union forces in the Indian Territory to make war on other tribes who had allied themselves with the South. Tired of the war, the Kickapoos had left their reservation and were heading for the peaceful environment of Mexico. They weren't looking for a fight, but they soundly defeated the Confederates in a daylong battle.

Returning Federal troops struggled with a growing lack of fresh water and firewood. The buildings were also in poor to crumbling down condition. The fort was abandoned in 1868.

Today the ruins of Fort Chadbourne are on private property, but the owner does permit nonstop drive-bys of the site. A state historical marker is located at the former cemetery of Fort Chadbourne, beside U.S. 277 ten miles north of Bronte.

U.S. Army Period (1848-1861)

Fort McKavett

Located on a limestone promontory overlooking the south bank of the San Saba River in 1852, the installation first bore the unofficial name of Camp San Saba during its first period of occupation. Several companies of infantry labored to construct buildings of stone, all roofed with wooden shingles. A two-story post commanders home, a general store, and a carpenters shop were erected, as were several barracks. All the while the garrison provided protection for frontier settlements in the region. In 1859 the post was abandoned because Indian raids had tapered off.

Confederate cavalry occupied the site in early 1862, confining many Union prisoners of war there and continually scouting and patrolling for hostile Indians. After only a few months the Confederates pulled out of the region, but long-range patrols often camped at the abandoned fort.

Most of the post was in ruins when Federal troops returned in 1868. Only the two-story post commander's home was relatively intact when units of the black 41st Infantry and 9th Cavalry arrived. The troops immediately began the rebuilding process of the newly named Fort McKavett, living in tents for the next year while the work was in progress. During this time they also performed their military duties, bringing the campaign to subdue the Kiowa and Comanche to the Indians' home territory. This second occupation of the fort resulted in the construction of four barracks, twelve officers quarters, a hospital, guardhouse, a headquarters building, powder magazine, a bakery, two storehouses, three stables, and a forage house. To top off this amazing construction project, a thirty-acre garden was tilled and planted.

By 1874 the power of the Kiowa and Comanche was beginning to fade after some stunning losses and the dogged pursuit of the army. The almost total completion of Fort McKavett also freed more soldiers, who had been acting as construction laborers, to take the field against the hostiles in the area. The reputation of the tough, aggressive buffalo soldier was well represented by the black troops of Fort McKavett. The early 1880s saw the Indians powerless to stop or even slow the advancing farms and settlements into what was once the untamed frontier. In 1883 Fort McKavett was abandoned, its military presence no longer needed.

Most of the fort's buildings were taken over by the townspeople of Fort McKavett, the town that had grown up around the fort and adopted its name. Unused structures were allowed to fall into ruin.

U.S. Army Period (1848-1861)

Later History

Today the surviving buildings of the fort form the nucleus of the town of Fort McKavett, its historic district. Other buildings have been restored by the state to form Fort McKavett State Historical Park, which opened to the public in 1968. At the site are the hospital, now housing interpretive exhibits about the fort, a schoolhouse, the bakery, one barracks, and the headquarters building. These structures are in good repair, as are four officers quarters that have been extensively altered from their original appearance. In ruins are the remaining barracks, some walls and fireplaces still standing, and the original post commanders house, which burned in 1942.

The town of Fort McKavett is on FM 864 just south of U.S. 190, west of Menard. The artifacts, exhibits, dioramas, and historical photos on display in the old hospital building can be viewed Wednesday through Sunday from 8 to 5.

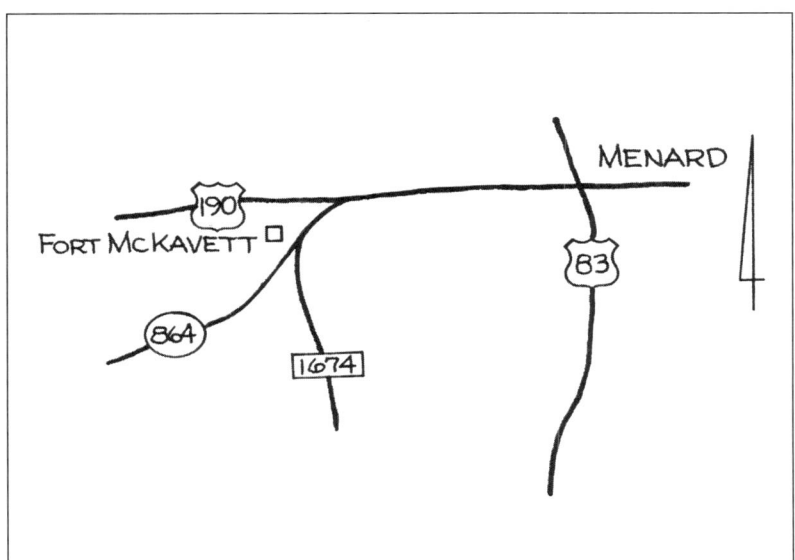

Fort Picketville

Founded in 1854 on Gonzales Creek, known then as Gunsolus Creek, it was named for either local rancher William Picket or for the building style used in constructing the houses. Picketville, as it was sometimes called, was used for collective defense by the local settlers through the 1850s and 1860s. It served as county seat for Stephens County from 1858 to 1864. The site was abandoned in the 1870s when the town of Breckenridge was named the new county seat.

When General Persifor F. Smith selected the site for Fort Davis in 1854, nobody agreed with his choice. Situated in a lush valley surrounded on three sides by high cliffs, the fort would have been vulnerable to attack by any enemy occupying the heights. Smith stood by his decision and construction on the fort, near Limpia Creek at the base of Sleeping Lion Mountain in the Davis Mountains, was begun. The high elevation of the site led many to comment that "the rest of Texas is downhill from here."

Fort Davis

Situated just over two hundred miles east of Fort Bliss in El Paso, Fort Davis stood along a line of forts constructed to protect the El Paso–San Antonio Road. In 1854 six companies of the Eighth Infantry arrived to build and garrison the new fort in the box canyon Smith had chosen. The unit commander, however, did not agree with the location and supervised the construction of shelters of a more temporary nature, hoping the fort would be relocated someday to a more favorable site

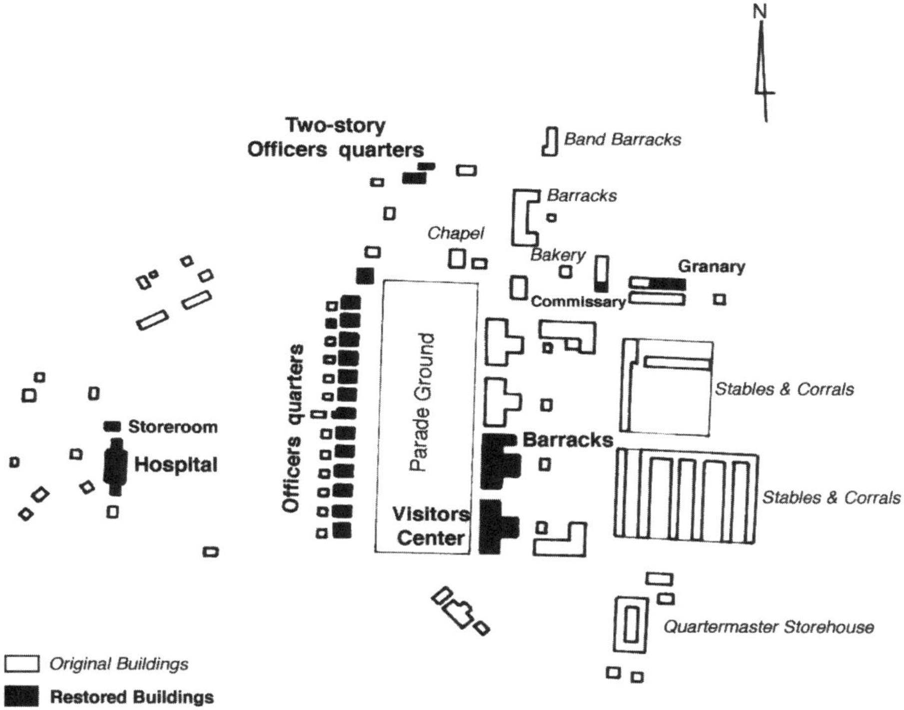

U.S. Army Period (1848-1861)

Officers quarters

**Fort Davis
Then and Now**

away from the surrounding cliffs. The buildings were of pine slab construction, sixty in all, scattered around the canyon in no particular pattern.

By 1856 six stone barracks had been erected in a line across the mouth of the canyon in the area the post commander had wanted the entire fort to be built. In a reversal of the military standards of the day, the enlisted men lived in the stone housing and the officers occupied the rickety wooden shanties in the canyon.

From Fort Davis the Eighth Infantry mounted patrols against Apache and Comanche raiders. On horseback and on foot, the soldiers rarely came to grips with the elusive warriors in any sort of pitched battle, and raids on freight wagons and settlers on the El Paso-San Antonio Road continued. At the onset of the Civil War the fort was abandoned by Federal troops and immediately taken over by Confederate forces in June of 1861. The Confederates performed the same guard and patrol duties the Union soldiers had previously.

The Confederate occupation of Fort Davis lasted only a year. In August of 1861 thirteen soldiers were ambushed by Apache raiders and all but one were killed. When a Confederate attempt to invade and take over New Mexico failed, the fort was abandoned in the spring of 1862 as the Southerners consolidated their forces in San Antonio. For the next five years the fort stood empty, the wooden shanties slowly dismantled by the Apaches for use as firewood. Two years after the end of the Civil War, Federal troops were again ordered into the area to regarrison Fort Davis. The soldiers that came were unlike any who had come before. They would soon begin to carve out a reputation for themselves that is still honored today.

Four companies of the Ninth Cavalry, a newly organized regiment of black soldiers, began reconstruction of the fort in

U.S. Army Period (1848-1861)

1867. The new site, on the plain outside the canyon near the existing stone barracks, was exactly where the former post commander of the Eighth Infantry had always envisioned it should be. The black soldiers, led by white officers by army policy, performed their duties admirably. They patrolled the El Paso-San Antonio Road, mounted expeditions against the Apache, and built most of the stone and adobe structures of the fort. Between 1867 and 1885 units of every black regiment in the army would be posted at Fort Davis. The Ninth and Tenth Cavalry regiments and Twenty-fourth and Twenty-fifth Infantry regiments all supplied troops to garrison the fort.

157

In the campaign of 1879-80 against the Apache leader Victorio and his warriors, the buffalo soldiers of Fort Davis played an integral role. In a series of sharply fought battles along the border, Victorio was prevented from reentering the United States from his stronghold in Mexico. He eventually was trapped and killed by Mexican soldiers because his escape routes into this country were blocked.

With the death of Victorio, peace finally came to the region of Fort Davis. Soldiers were kept at their previous duties of patrols, parade drills, and road and telegraph repair. The threat of Apache attack had been eliminated for good. In 1885 the black troops of Fort Davis were transferred to New Mexico, where they campaigned against the last Apache leader Geronimo. The military need for the fort had come to an end, and in 1891 the post was officially abandoned by the army.

Later History

When Fort Davis was abandoned, it boasted an impressive array of buildings, over fifty in all. There were quarters for twelve companies, including several company-sized barracks. Each of these buildings was twenty-seven feet by one hundred eighty-six feet in dimension and contained two large squad rooms, a kitchen, mess, and storeroom. There were also sergeants quarters and offices inside.

Separate officers quarters, nineteen total, were single-story buildings with front and back porches. Each home consisted of a bedroom and sitting room, divided from each other by a central fireplace and chimney.

There was also a bakery at Fort Davis, a blacksmith shop, a carpenters shed, commissary, chapel, hospital, and two stables.

U.S. Army Period (1848-1861)

In 1961 Congress authorized the establishment of the Fort Davis National Historic Site under the jurisdiction of the National Park Service. More than half of the original structures were restored on the 460-acre park site now located just over twenty miles from the towns of Marfa and Alpine.

Today Fort Davis is considered the best surviving example of a late nineteenth-century military post in the Southwest. Five of the twenty-five restored buildings are furnished with period furniture, including one barracks building. The museum and visitors center also houses a bookstore. The fort is located on the north edge of the small town of Fort Davis on State Highways 17-118, and access to the site is by personal vehicle only; no public transportation is available. During the

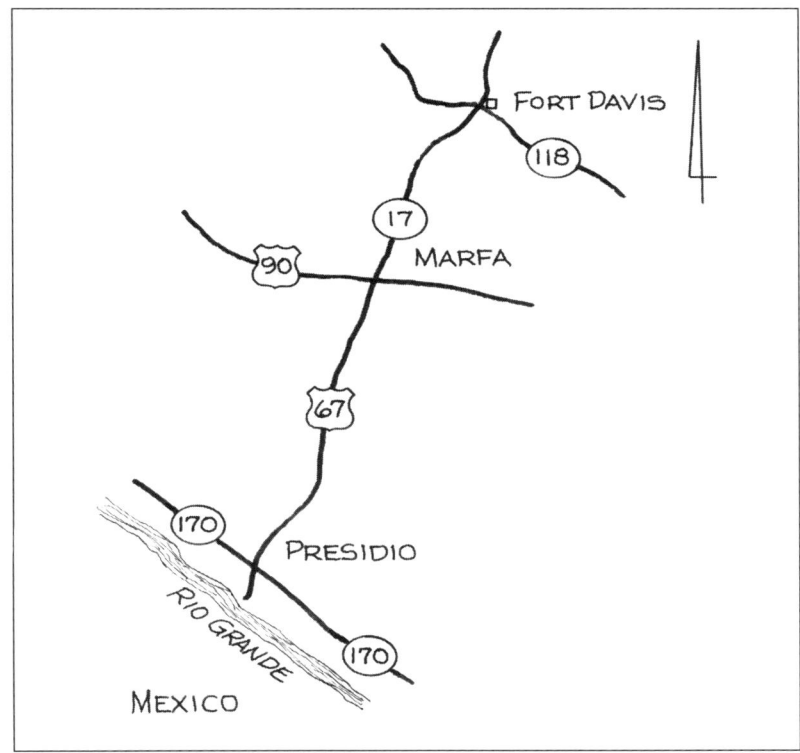

summer costumed interpreters conduct tours and give demonstrations; other times tours are self-conducted.

Fort Davis National Historic Site is open daily. Summer hours are from 8 to 6 and winter hours are 8 A.M. to 5 P.M. It is closed only on Christmas Day. Admission is $2.00 per person, children 16 and under admitted free.

Camp Verde, three miles from Bandera Pass in the Texas Hill Country, was the site of one of the most interesting experiments the frontier army ever conducted.

Camp Verde

Established on the banks of Verde Creek in 1855, the camp became home for forty camels. Imported, with Arab handlers, the beasts were an attempt to curb transportation costs associated with hauling supplies by horse, mule, and oxen. The camels, however, scared every four-legged creature they encountered and proved too much to handle for the soldiers assigned the duty of working with them. By the time of the Civil War, the experiment in camel transport had failed and the animals had been abandoned to make their own way in the wild.

In 1861 Confederate forces captured Camp Verde and rounded up almost eighty camels from the surrounding countryside. They used the animals to haul cotton south to Mexico to exchange for needed supplies. The Confederates also patrolled the region, keeping the Indians in check throughout the war, and oversaw the operation of a prisoner-of-war camp containing up to 600 Union captives in a nearby canyon.

U.S. Army Period (1848-1861)

When the Civil War ended, Union troops again occupied Camp Verde, and the camels were allowed to run wild once more. Many of the animals were later rounded up and sold to a circus. From 1865 on, the post was gradually phased out until its final abandonment in 1869. A company of Texas Rangers would eventually take over the site before they, too, moved on. As late as 1949 remains of camel corrals could be found there.

A state historical marker indicates the location of Camp Verde. The marker is thirteen miles south of Kerrville on a farm road a half mile from SH 173 South.

Fort Lancaster

Established in 1855 on the east bank of Live Oak Creek a half mile north of its junction with the Pecos River, the fort's first structures were crude log shelters that were soon replaced by more permanent stone or adobe buildings. By 1860 more than twenty-nine buildings had been erected and occupied, including barracks, kitchens, blacksmith shop, bakery, and hospital. Members of the 1st Infantry, mounted on mules, protected wagon trains on the "lower road" portion of the road from San Antonio to El Paso.

When Fort Lancaster was abandoned by Federal forces in 1861, it was only briefly taken over by the Confederates. The Confederate soldiers left in early 1862, and it was not until 1871 that Federal troops returned to the post. By 1874 Fort Lancaster was abandoned for good.

Later History

The state of Texas acquired eighty-one acres of land in 1968 from private owners and Crockett County for use as a state park. Most, but not all, of the ruins of Fort Lancaster were included. In 1975 forty-one more acres were donated to the state that contained more ruins.

Visible remains at Fort Lancaster State Historic Site include building foundations, a chimney, wall sections from six to ten feet in height, a lime kiln, a cemetery, and some trash dumps. A modern visitors and interpretive center, including a Texas state park store with bookstore and gifts, is open from Memorial Day to Labor Day 9 A.M. to 6 P.M., and the rest of the year Thursday through Monday 9 A.M. to 5 P.M. The park is located off exit 343 of Interstate 10, on Highway 290 eight miles east of Sheffield.

U.S. Army Period (1848-1861)

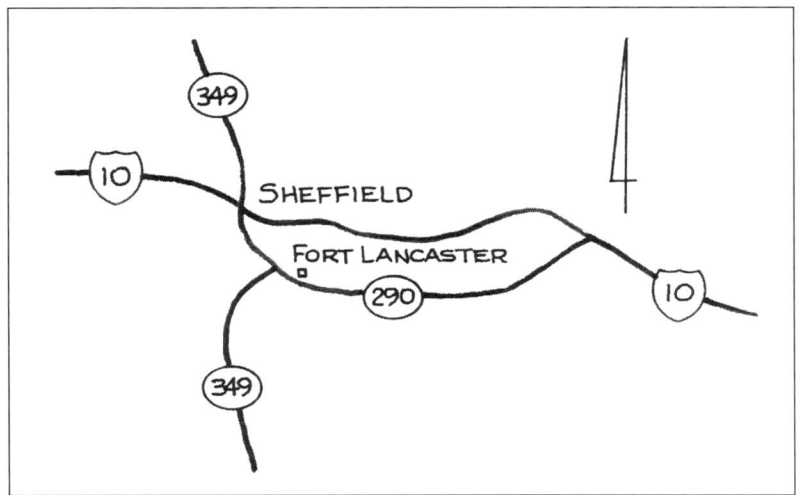

Camp Cooper

This site was built on the Clear Fork of the Brazos River in 1856, near the future site of Fort Griffin (1867). The first commander of the camp was Lt. Col. Robert E. Lee, serving from 1856 to 1857, leading four companies of the 2nd Cavalry. The camp suffered from extremes of weather and infestations of insects, but the most dangerous nuisance were the rattlesnakes that frequented the site. Until his transfer in 1857, Lee even kept one as a pet.

Structures at the camp were of stone, mud brick, and wood picket construction. They included barracks, officers quarters, a hospital, and a commissary. From this base, troops campaigned against the Comanche and were instrumental in the killing of Chief Peta Nocona in 1860 and the capture of his white wife, Cynthia Ann Parker. Parker had been abducted from her home, Fort Parker, in 1836 at the age of nine. She was raised as a Comanche, married Peta Nocona, and bore him three children. Her son Quanah Parker would become the last great Comanche chief.

Camp Cooper was surrendered to Confederate forces in 1861 and after the war was not reoccupied by Federal troops.

Fort Hudson

This fort was built on San Pedro Creek, a tributary of Devils River, in 1857, on the road between San Antonio and El Paso. The out-of-the-way location chosen for the fort, an elevated site well away from the road, meant few visitors and no town constructed nearby. The loneliness of the post was offset by the construction of comfortable quarters. Using a mixture of gravel and lime, the buildings' walls were built up slowly in layers. The resulting structures were cool in the summer and warm in the winter. The fort also had its own post office.

When the Federals abandoned the fort in 1861, Confederate troops of the 2nd Texas Cavalry used the site as a supply base for incursions into New Mexico. The Confederates withdrew from Fort Hudson in 1862, but the post was not reoccupied by Union troops until 1867 after a stagecoach was ambushed nearby by Indians and two soldiers riding escort were killed.

U.S. Army Period (1848-1861)

For the next ten years the troops from Fort Hudson waged successful campaigns against the local Indian tribes, even pursuing them into Mexico to do battle. So successful were the troopers that by early 1877 there was virtually no further threat of Indian raids in the area, and the fort was abandoned.

In 1936 a historical marker was placed at the site of Fort Hudson. By 1980 all the comfortable buildings of the fort, now situated on private property, had crumbled to dust.

Fort Cibolo

Another example of a private fortress-home was built in 1857 on Cibolo Creek by Milton Faver. Faver was a combination rancher, farmer, and trader, and his homestead covered some 2,880 acres of land along the north side of the Rio Grande. His first, or main, house was known as El Fortin del Cibolo, the Fort of the Buffalo, and was ninety feet wide by one hundred sixty feet long. This massive adobe structure had walls twenty feet high and three to four feet thick, studded with broken glass to prevent an attacker from attempting to climb them. Gun ports were all along the walls to allow easy firing at any enemy outside. The interior rooms all opened onto a central courtyard, and at the northwest and southeast corners of the house were two circular towers. A 140-foot stone walled corral adjoined the house.

Sixteen miles from the main house, Faver built El Fortin de la Cienega, the Fort of the Marshy Place, a smaller fortified house that served as the headquarters for his cattle ranching. Four miles further on was built El Fortin la Morita, the Fort of the Little Mulberry Tree, a fortified cottage that was headquarters for his sheep and goat herding operation. In all, Faver had over sixty employees living and working out of the main house and twenty others out of the other two houses. He and his family, a wife and son, lived comfortably at Fort Cibolo.

Passing military units from Fort Davis often quartered at Fort Cibolo while out on patrol, and Faver kept up a lively trade with the post. He provided Fort Davis with beef, mutton, fruits, and vegetables. He also provided peach brandy, produced from his own still. He sold his brandy not only to the army but also traded it with local Indians for hides and horses. When Federal troops withdrew from the area during

U.S. Army Period (1848-1861)

the Civil War and hard-pressed Confederate troops failed to provide adequate protection from increased Indian raids, Faver and his men stood alone. The Fort Cibolo complex proved equal to the task and resisted all attacks and raids successfully.

After the war Federal troops from Fort Davis supplied Fort Cibolo with a cannon for defense in return for allowing a detachment of men to be quartered there on a permanent basis and supplies to be stored there. When Faver died in 1889, he left his estate to be divided evenly between his wife and son. The son was adjudged to be incompetent to handle his share of the wealth and property his father had accumulated, and the widow sold off all the livestock and gave the money to a faith healer. The Fort Cibolo complex was sold off piecemeal, and the abandoned houses fell into disrepair.

Later History

By the 1970s the site of Fort Cibolo was open ranchland owned by J.E. White and Sons Ranch. In 1990 the property was purchased by John Poindexter, who began the process of restoring the old buildings to their former appearance. It was his intention to turn the site into a vacation resort to be called Cibolo Creek Ranch.

Using old photographs, written and oral descriptions, and a variety of archival materials, Poindexter oversaw the restorations with an eye for authenticity. All modern upgrades—electricity, plumbing, and air conditioning—were cleverly concealed within new construction that imitated old techniques. Additionally, a museum was set up on the lower floor of the southeast tower at the main house, and several other rooms display artifacts and weaponry from the history of Fort Cibolo and the region.

Cibolo Creek Ranch is a private facility. The main house, El Fortin del Cibolo, offers eleven rooms for rent; prices are based on double occupancy with meals included. El Fortin de la Cienega, also with a small museum, offers four rooms. Both houses have heated pools and other amenities. La Morita is a two-room house with one bedroom and no electricity. Meals are delivered or can be enjoyed at the main house. A variety of outdoor activities are available to guests, from hiking to horseback riding.

The ranch is located thirty-three miles south of Marfa and twenty-five miles north of Presidio on U.S. 67.

U.S. Army Period (1848-1861)

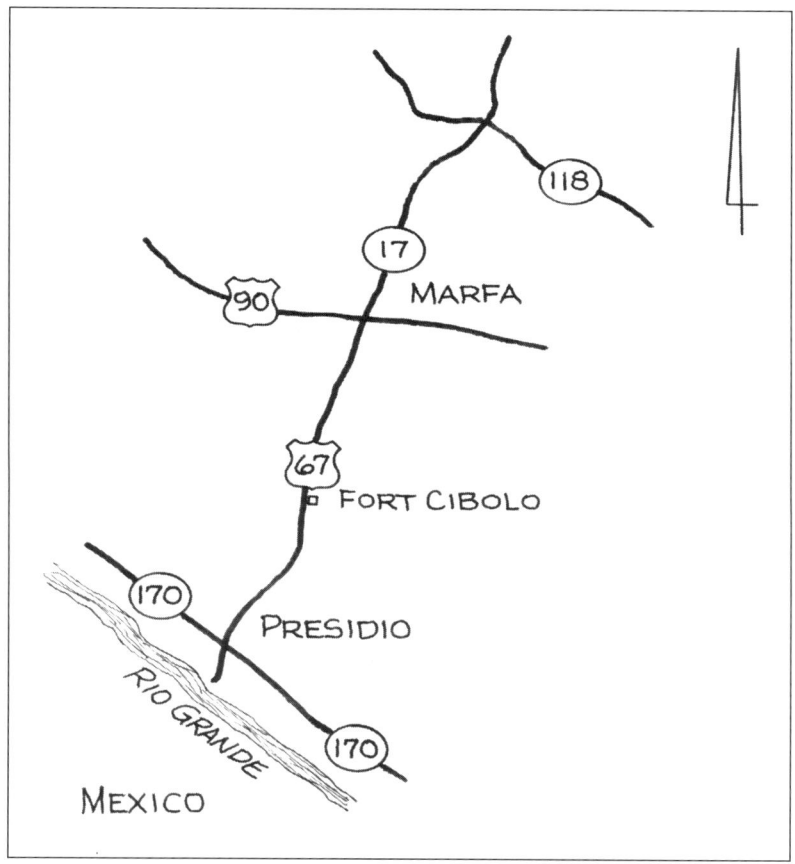

In West Texas, Comanche Springs is the main source of water in the area and the third largest springs in the state. It is no wonder, then, that the U.S. Army would choose the site for a major military installation in the 1800s.

Fort Stockton

Originally called Camp Stockton, the post was established in 1858 to protect the numerous travelers drawn to the abundant supply of water in the arid territory. In 1859 the Butterfield-Overland Mail began regular stagecoach runs through the area. Many roads and trails led to or passed through the Camp Stockton site, including a Comanche war trail. This Comanche travel way kept the soldiers stationed at Stockton, men of the 1st and 8th Infantry, busy guarding roads and travelers from attack.

In 1861 Federal troops were withdrawn and Confederate forces occupied the fort. Elements of the 2nd Regiment Texas Mounted Rifles were stationed at Camp Stockton only briefly, abandoning the post in 1862. When the Civil War ended in 1865, nothing remained of the facility.

Four companies of the 9th U.S. Cavalry, a regiment of black soldiers, reestablished Fort Stockton in 1867. The new location, under its new name, was one-half mile northeast of the first site and was situated on a 960-acre parcel leased from civilian landowners. Construction of permanent facilities of stone and adobe began immediately after the troops' arrival, and a small town sprang up nearby.

From 1867 to 1886 elements of every black regiment in the army were stationed at Fort Stockton. In fact, 87 percent of all soldiers posted at the fort throughout its active service were buffalo soldiers, a name given the black troopers by

U.S. Army Period (1848-1861)

their Indian adversaries. Despite difficult living conditions, harsh duty assignments, and local prejudices, the black soldiers had lower incidents of alcoholism and desertions than any white unit in the army. Trouble did, however, occasionally occur.

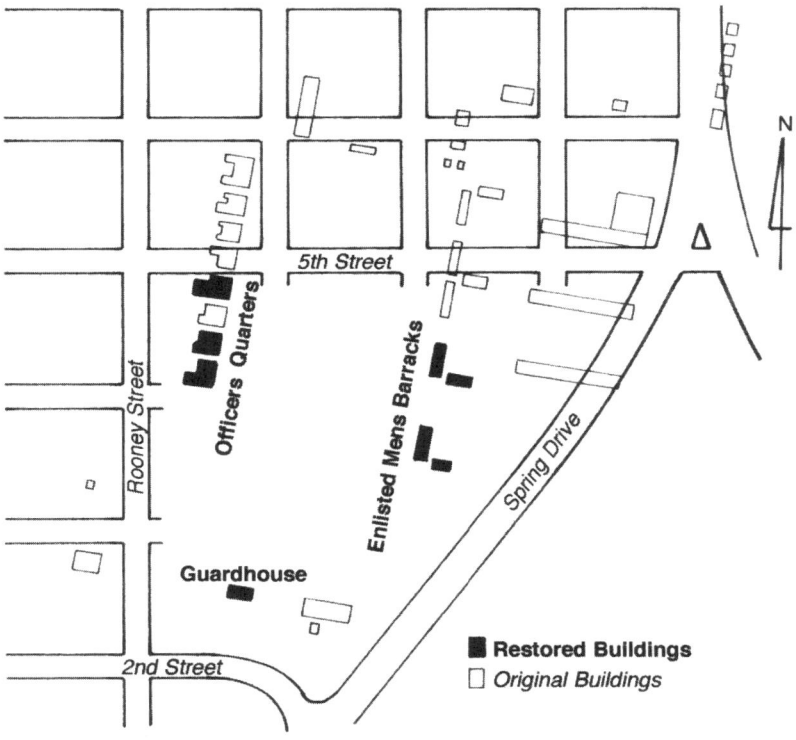

Fort Stockton Then and Now

An Illustrated History of Texas Forts

In 1873 a black trooper reported to the fort's white doctor for morning sick call. The doctor gave the soldier some medicine and ordered him back to duty. Each morning for the next three days, the trooper reported for sick call and the doctor refused to excuse him from his daily duty assignments. On the third morning the doctor had the soldier arrested and confined in the guardhouse, charging him with being a malingerer attempting to shirk his duties. The trooper died in confinement the next day.

U.S. Army Period (1848-1861)

There was an understandable feeling of outrage among the black garrison. A petition was circulated blaming the doctor for the trooper's death and calling for his removal from the position he held. Some soldiers openly called for a mutiny against their white officers if their demands were not met. Unfortunately, the army would tolerate a certain amount of discontent from the enlisted men—it was to be expected—but talk of insurrection was not taken lightly. Any soldier who had spoken of such an action was promptly arrested, court-martialed, and sentenced to anywhere from five to fifteen years in prison.

Despite that one incident, the black soldiers at Fort Stockton performed their duties with a high degree of enthusiasm and pride. But by 1886 the frontier had moved further west and the Indian threat had been eliminated. Fort Stockton was no longer needed and was abandoned.

Later History

When Fort Stockton was abandoned, it consisted of thirty-five buildings, most of adobe and two of limestone construction. Residents of the town of Fort Stockton that had been built up around the post simply moved into many of the fort's buildings. Others dismantled the remaining buildings for construction materials. Unused structures fell into disrepair and eventually disappeared, victims of neglect and the elements.

What remains today of the Fort Stockton post are three officers quarters, the infamous guardhouse, and two enlisted men barracks with accompanying kitchen buildings. All are centrally located within the city of Fort Stockton and are listed in the National Register of Historic Sites as The Fort Stockton Historic District. The site is located along Interstate

10 at westbound exit 261 or eastbound exits 256, 257, and 259.

Of the three officers quarters, OQ #7 has been restored and furnished to its 1870s appearance, one room left bare and unplastered to reveal construction techniques of the period. The Historic Fort Stockton Museum is located in Enlisted Mans Barracks #1 and showcases exhibits of everyday life at the fort. The hours of operation of the museum are Monday through Saturday 10 A.M. to 5 P.M. In the summer the hours are Monday through Saturday 10 A.M. to 8 P.M. and Sunday 1 P.M. to 5 P.M. Admission is charged.

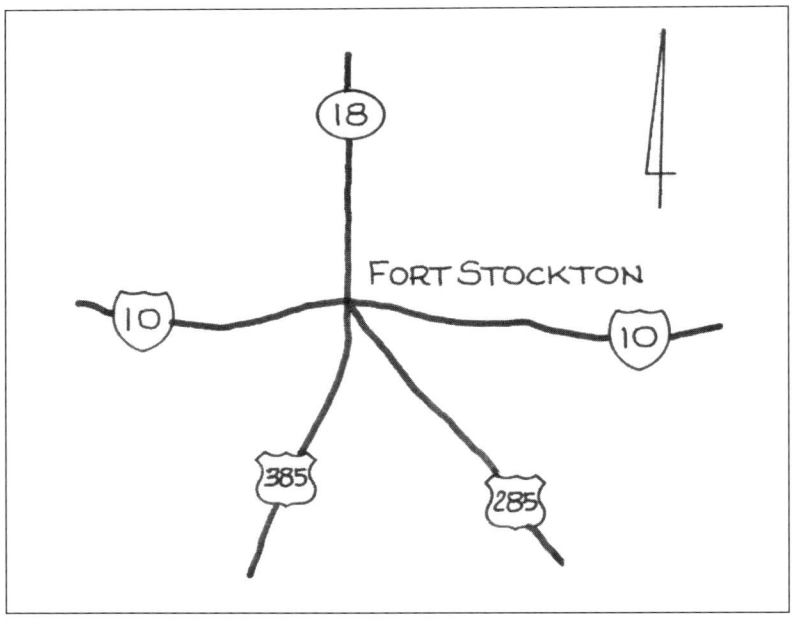

U.S. Army Period (1848-1861)

Fort Quitman

Established on a barren, sandy stretch of land eighty miles southeast of El Paso in 1858, Fort Quitman easily won the distinction of being the most uncomfortable post in Texas. Only 400 yards east of the Rio Grande, the fort nevertheless suffered from the hot, dry climate and sandy soil conditions in which nothing would grow. Subsequently, all supplies had to be shipped in at inflated prices. Fort Quitman was situated on the El Paso-San Antonio Road and was charged with guarding wagon trains and travelers from Apache, Comanche, and Mexican bandit alike. This assignment was made all the more difficult by the fact that the troops stationed there were infantrymen. A few adobe structures were built, but they offered no real protection from the searing heat and harsh elements.

The Federals cheerfully abandoned Fort Quitman at the outbreak of the Civil War. Even though the fort occupied a position on the line of supply and communication for the Confederate invasion of New Mexico from Texas, it was never fully garrisoned by them. Union troops from California did occupy the fort briefly in 1862 but soon headed back to the West Coast. After that the Confederates contented themselves with stripping all the wood from the fort.

In 1868 units of the 9th Cavalry returned to reoccupy Fort Quitman. The adobe buildings still stood but were devoid of roofs, windows, window frames, doorframes, and doors. The troopers labored mightily to repair the old buildings and erect new ones. By 1876 Fort Quitman consisted of two company-sized barracks, five buildings containing two officers quarters each, a guardhouse, a bakery, some workshops, two storehouses, and a stable.

In typical military fashion, Fort Quitman was ordered abandoned in 1877, just a year after its completion. But it was regarrisoned in 1880 as a subpost of Fort Davis during the campaign against the Apache leader Victorio. By 1882 the fort was abandoned for good, and the desert scoured the area clean, leaving no trace of Fort Quitman today.

Confederate Period

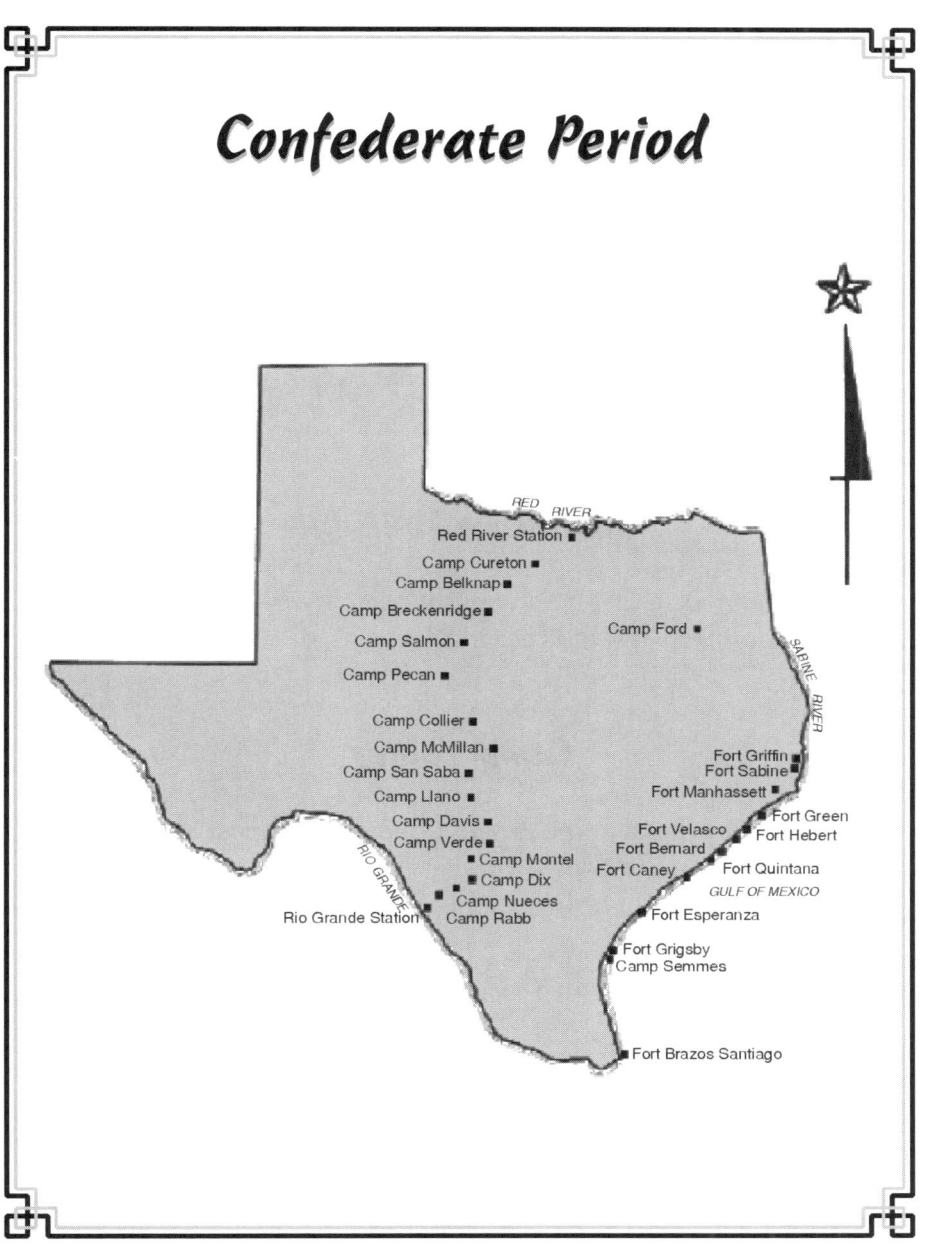

At the onset of the Civil War, Federal troops were hastily withdrawn from Texas. Confederate troops simply moved into the abandoned forts and assumed the protective duties of their predecessors. Additionally, a line of camps was established from the Red River to the Rio Grande diagonally across the center of Texas. These camps were a day's ride apart, and from there regular patrols were sent out to curb Indian raids, round up Confederate draft dodgers, and capture deserters. Little if any trace of those camps remain today, but state historical markers note many former locations.

Camp Breckenridge

Marker located on the southwest corner of Courthouse Square on U.S. 180 in Breckenridge.

Camp Collier

Marker located at the Brown County courthouse on Broadway and Center in Brownwood.

Camp Cureton

Marker located on courthouse lawn on Center Street, Highway 79, in Archer City.

Camp Dix

Marker located at the corner of Main Street, U.S. 90, and Getty on the Town Plaza in Uvalde.

Camp McMillan

Marker located on the courthouse grounds off Highway 190 in San Saba.

Camp Montel

Marker located at 504 Main Street, Highway 16, in Bandera.

Camp Nueces

Marker located in a roadside park eight to ten miles north of La Pryor on Highway 83.

Camp Pecan

Marker located on the courthouse grounds off Highway 20 Business in Baird.

Camp Rabb

Marker located in front of Chamber of Commerce on Garrison Street, near the bridges to Mexico in El Paso.

Red River Station

Marker located on U.S. 82, six miles west of Nacona.

Camp Salmon

Marker located on the north side of the courthouse lawn off Main Street in Eastland.

Camp San Saba

Marker located off U.S. 87 on FM 1955, ten miles south of Brady.

Camp Verde

Marker located on the southwest corner of the courthouse grounds at Sidney Baker and Main in Kerrville.

Camp Llano and Camp Davis

No markers located.

Confederate Period

Blair's Fort

Constructed in 1860 on the ranch of C.C. Blair by at least eight local families as a communal protection from Comanche and Tonkawa raiders, this "family fort" had twelve log cabins measuring fourteen square feet apiece arranged in two parallel rows. Each cabin was fourteen feet from its neighbor, and picket walls, eight to ten feet high, were erected between the buildings. Within the compound was stored enough ammunition and supplies to withstand a prolonged siege if the need arose.

Blair's Fort was occupied from 1861 to 1865. After the Civil War, units of the Texas Rangers used the fort as a frequent stopover point while on their patrols. The fort was no longer occupied as a defensive position by that time by area settlers, and the site remained abandoned, falling into decay.

Originally intended as a training facility for Confederate conscripts, Camp Ford was pressed into service as a P.O.W. camp within a year of its establishment and continued to function in that capacity until the end of the Civil War.

Camp Ford

Located in East Texas near the present-day city of Tyler, Camp Ford was built in 1862 on the top and slope of a ridge. A spring-fed creek at the base of the ridge supplied water for the installation. As a training facility, the camp had adequate shelter and space for the troops assigned there. The situation changed in July of 1863 when 100 Union prisoners were sent to the camp, with an additional 400 arriving in November.

Up to 600 slaves were put to work to build a walled enclosure, surrounding a three-acre site, to contain the prisoners. Logs were cut and split to eighteen-foot lengths and set in trenches three to four feet deep. In just ten days the slaves completed their task, and the prisoners began building their own shelters inside the new stockade. Quarters for the Confederate guards were built outside the south and west walls. The spring-fed creek wound up inside the south wall, where the prisoners had access to it. Conditions were comparatively good within the stockade for the captives, the area being more than able to accommodate their numbers without overcrowding.

But in the spring of 1864 the Union suffered major defeats on the battlefield in Arkansas and Louisiana. More than 4,000 Federals were captured. To handle such a large number of prisoners, Camp Ford was expanded from its original three acres to almost sixteen.

Confederate Period

Once again an army of slaves bent their backs to the task. To rapidly obtain the timber needed to enclose the new camp, the top half of the logs along the south and west walls were sawed off and the logs from the north and west walls were removed, cut in half, and reset. In a Herculean effort the new stockade was erected in just three days. The newly arrived prisoners then set about building their own quarters inside from logs, brush, and clay. Even at its increased size, Camp Ford was crowded, but there is no evidence of mistreatment or abuse by the guards.

In fact, at the war's end in 1865, the former prisoners and guards celebrated together, along with local citizens who came to the camp to attend a giant rummage sale. Camp Ford was abandoned in May of 1865 and virtually disappeared as civilians carried away all the cut logs from the walls and buildings.

Later History

The land upon which Camp Ford once stood was cultivated and farmed until the early 1940s, when portions of the ridge it had occupied were mechanically terraced and planted with pine, oak, and other hardwood trees. Earlier, around 1925, the spring-fed creek had been diverted and developed as a recreational site that operated until the early 1950s. Further landscaping of the area in the 1960s destroyed much of the evidence of the northern portion of the expanded stockade.

In 1989-90 the Smith County Historical Society conducted field studies at the Camp Ford site. Much evidence concerning the fort's layout was unearthed, as well as many artifacts from the Civil War period. In 1997 the Center for Ecological Archaeology at Texas A&M University conducted its own investigation. Controlled digs, aerial photography, and side-scanning radar have produced an accurate picture of the original Camp Ford. Field investigations of the site are continuing today.

Confederate Period

Fort Waul

Construction began on the fort in 1863, using largely slave labor. Located on a high, wide hill, known locally as Waldrip Hill, the fort overlooked the town of Gonzales to the south and was intended for use as a supply depot and defensive position on the Guadalupe River.

Massive earthen walls were built up eight feet high and four to six feet thick at the top. The base of the walls was twelve feet thick. A stone blockhouse was located in the center of the enclosure, and bastions for cannons were planned for each corner of the walls. A defensive ditch, eight feet wide and four feet deep, was begun outside the western wall but never completed. Into 1864 construction continued, but the fortunes of war had already turned against the Confederacy.

In late 1864 the fort was abruptly abandoned in the face of dwindling supplies and the lack of any Union activity to defend against. It was left incomplete and unnamed.

Later History

By the late 1870s the central blockhouse had all but vanished, local citizens carting away the stones for other uses. But the site did finally receive the name of Fort Waul, after a Confederate general who had once lived nearby.

The site today is in the care of the Gonzales County Historical Committee but is not open to the general public, even though most of the outer walls, measuring some 250 feet by 750 feet, and a portion of the defensive ditch remain.

During the latter years of the Civil War, civilians banded together to build protective communities, or family forts, to safeguard themselves and their families from Indian raids. Inadequate protection from Confederate forces, undermanned and stretched too thin over large areas, made "forting up" on the Texas frontier necessary for survival.

Davis Family Fort

Built on a level, circular terrace above the Clear Fork of the Brazos River, Fort Davis was named after the president of the Confederacy, Jefferson Davis, in 1864. Several families came together to construct over twenty log houses at the site of an existing one-story sandstone block building. The 24-foot-by-44-foot stone house predated the fort by several years.

By 1865 the picket log structures formed a defensive rectangle that measured 300 feet by 325 feet with a central travel way running lengthwise through it. Plans for blockhouses at each corner of the rectangle and a perimeter wall to enclose the area were never implemented. Portions of the wall were erected, but no complete enclosure was effected. This fort was not actually designed to withstand a concentrated military assault but to provide protective quarters for men and their families to defend themselves in large numbers instead of individually from the Indians' hit-and-run form of warfare.

At the end of the Civil War, the U.S. Army returned to Texas and undertook the establishment of many new frontier forts. Families at the Davis Family Fort returned to their more isolated homesteads, and by 1867 only the stone house remained. Since all other construction at the site had been of wood, either the elements had brought the structures down or new settlers raided them for building materials. A nearby cemetery, some 400 yards northeast of the stone house, held the remains of individuals interred there while the fort was occupied. In later years individuals who had once occupied the fort and moved away would wind up buried in the fort's cemetery also.

Later History

Today the stone house and the cemetery are all that remain of the Davis Family Fort. In 1991 archaeological studies at the site uncovered a wealth of artifacts dating to the fort's construction and use. The stone house, used more recently as a hunting lodge, has been remodeled to accommodate such conveniences as an interior bathroom, electricity, and a screened-in porch. A center wall that divided the house into two rooms has been removed to create one large open area inside.

The site of the Davis Family Fort is approximately seventeen miles northeast of Albany and fifteen miles north-northwest of Breckenridge.

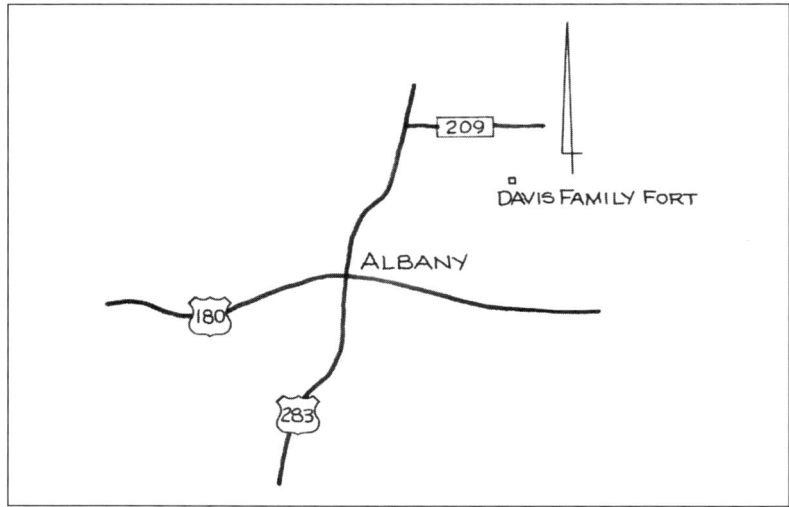

With the threat of Union invasion from the sea and hundreds of miles of coastline to defend, Texas Confederates constructed a series of forts at strategic points at and along navigable rivers that could be accessed from the Gulf of Mexico. Many of these coastal forts would be abandoned in favor of better positions, some would see no conflict, and still others would be the site of sharp engagements with the Union army and navy.

Fort Sabine

The citizens of the town of Sabine Pass, fifteen miles south of Port Arthur on the Sabine River, decided in 1862 to build a fort to protect their town in case of a Union invasion coming upriver. Using slave labor and their own muscle, the residents constructed an earth and timber emplacement commanding the river and mounted several cannon there. At least two of their cannon were thirty-two-pounders.

At first the post was garrisoned by the local militia, but they were soon replaced by regular Confederate troops of the 6th Texas Infantry. In September of 1862 what the townspeople had feared seemed about to happen. Union gunboats steamed up the Sabine River and shelled Fort Sabine. The defenders put up what resistance they could until the ships finally withdrew back down river.

Though no invasion force followed, the fort was heavily damaged in the exchange. An epidemic of yellow fever had broken out just before the gunboats arrived, so no repairs to the position were undertaken. The healthy members of the garrison simply spiked the guns and abandoned the fort, their ailing comrades in tow.

Fort Sabine was never reoccupied, even though the Sabine Pass area was a hotbed of activity. Instead, a new fort was constructed a mile or so away to the north at a better location. The two thirty-two-pounders from Fort Sabine were later moved to the new fort after being put back in working order.

The former site of Fort Sabine is now located off State Highway 87 on Farm Road 3322, one mile south of the Sabine Pass Battlefield State Historical Park.

Buffalo Springs

Situated near a line of Confederate outposts in North Texas that were established in the years 1861-65, this installation was also used as a family fort by local civilians using the "safety in numbers" type of defense. The picket log houses erected at the site were used primarily by Confederate cavalry units as a base of operations against Indians and Union troops moving down from Oklahoma. The position was abandoned in 1862 and later used as a stagecoach depot by the U.S. Army.

Confederate Period

Site of perhaps the greatest victory against overwhelming odds in Texas since Houston's rout of Santa Anna at San Jacinto in 1836, the battle of Sabine Pass at Fort Griffin won honors for its tiny garrison and turned away a Union invasion fleet.

Fort Griffin

After the bombardment and abandonment of Fort Sabine, another installation on the Sabine River was urgently needed. In March of 1863, 500 slaves labored to construct an earth and log fort on a high point of ground overlooking the river. The fort was triangular in shape, each side about 100 feet long, the sloping walls ten feet in height, and the parapet twenty feet wide. Beneath the parapet were the arsenal and bombproof shelters, reinforced with timbers and railroad rails. The river-facing wall had a saw-toothed top, through which the fort's six cannon could fire.

The armament of Fort Griffin consisted of two twenty-four-pound cannon, the two thirty-two-pounders from Fort Sabine, and two thirty-two-pound howitzers. Since most were smoothbore guns and not that accurate, the gunners practiced daily while the fort was still under construction. They sighted the guns on aiming stakes driven into the river channel, a move that would produce spectacular results in a very short time. In September of 1863 the anticipated Union invasion force finally arrived.

The Union fleet consisted of four light draft gunboats and twenty-two transport ships carrying approximately 5,000 troops. The garrison at Fort Griffin numbered just forty-two men. The Union gunboat *Clifton*, a 210-foot side-wheel steamer, moved up the Sabine River on the morning of September 8 and lobbed twenty-six shells at Fort Griffin from her

eight cannon. The guns of the fort remained silent. The *Clifton* was then joined by the other gunboats, *Sachem*, *Arizona*, and *Granite City*, followed by seven transport ships carrying 1,200 men. The rest of the fleet waited at the mouth of the river. By 3:30 in the afternoon all the ships were in position, the gunboats ready to bombard the fort while the transports landed troops for a ground assault. The guns of Fort Griffin had remained silent the whole time.

But when the Union gunboats reached the aiming stakes in the river channel, the guns of Fort Griffin roared out their greeting. The *Sachem*, also a steamship, took a shot to her boiler steam drum that scalded most of her crew with hot water and steam. Veering away from the deadly fire from Fort Griffin, the *Sachem* ran aground and immediately hoisted a white flag.

Meanwhile, the *Clifton* had her tiller ropes shot away and drifted out of control. With guns still blazing away at the fort, *Clifton* also ran aground and took heavy punishment from Fort Griffin. Most of her guns were disabled, and her boiler exploded from a direct hit before her crew abandoned ship.

By now the *Arizona* and *Granite City* were backing down river out of range, as were the still fully loaded transport ships, and the Battle of Sabine Pass was over. In less than an hour the gallant men of Fort Griffin had disabled and captured two Union gun ships, killed or wounded nearly 100 men, and taken 300 prisoners, all without losing a man killed or wounded. As if that were not accomplishment enough, two of their only six cannon had been disabled early in the exchange of fire with the gunboats.

The Union invasion fleet turned back to New Orleans, their starting point, tossing wagons, ammunition, rations, artillery, and hundreds of horses and mules overboard into the Gulf to lighten their load and gain more speed.

The garrison at Fort Griffin was immediately reinforced and its firepower increased by the addition of captured Union guns. But the Union never returned in strength to carry out an invasion or seek revenge for their terrible loss, and in 1865 Confederate forces spiked the cannons for the last time and abandoned the fort.

Later History

Rechannelization of the Sabine River over the years, coupled with large amounts of erosion, has destroyed the exact location of Fort Griffin. However, a statue of its commander,

Lt. Richard (Dick) Dowling, and a plaque mark what might have been the site of the fort. Statue and plaque are located in Sabine Pass Battleground State Historical Park. The park offers camping, picnicking, boating, and fishing and is just off State Highway 87, fifteen miles south of Port Arthur.

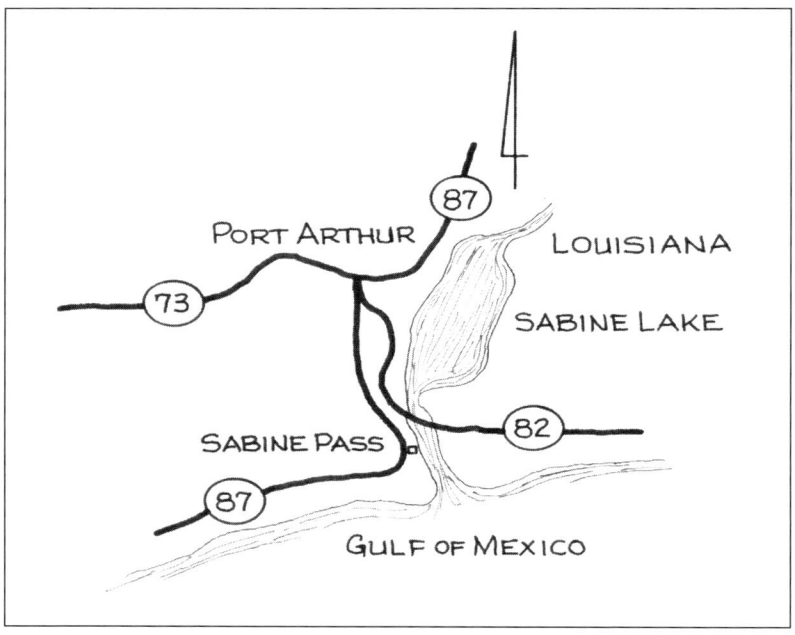

Fort Grigsby

Built on Grigsby's Bluff overlooking the Neches River in 1862, this post consisted of mud and clamshell embankments reinforced by upright logs sharpened to points. Fort Grigsby was armed with two twenty-four-pound cannon that commanded a bend in the river below. The fort was abandoned in 1863 without ever having fired a shot in anger.

Fort Manhassett

After the Battle of Sabine Pass at Fort Griffin in 1863, Confederate leaders still feared a return of the Union invasion fleet. They determined to build a new fort inland of Fort Griffin to prevent Union ground forces from flanking that position and perhaps continuing on overland to the town of Beaumont.

Fort Manhassett was a series of five earthen redoubts built on ridges west of the town of Sabine Pass. Seven companies of soldiers manned the position in 1863, armed with eight cannon. But no further Union threat ever presented itself, and when Fort Griffin was abandoned in 1865, so was Fort Manhassett.

Later archaeological excavations at the site revealed buried gunpowder and shells the Confederates could not carry away. A plaque now marks the location of Fort Manhassett, six miles west of Sabine Pass near State Highway 87.

Camp Semmes

Constructed on the southwestern end of St. Joseph Island near the town of Aransas in 1861, the artillery outpost of Camp Semmes was positioned to guard the naval approaches to Corpus Christi on the mainland. In 1862 Union troops landed on the island and captured the town and fort. They were driven away by a sharply fought counterattack. Returning in 1863 the Federals again captured the town of Aransas and Camp Semmes. This time, though, they burned everything to the ground before they withdrew, leaving no trace of the town or post. Neither was ever rebuilt.

Fort Quintana

Located on the west side of the mouth of the Brazos River, Fort Quintana overlooked a dam placed across the mouth of the river to prevent Union gunboats from sailing upstream. When the gunboats eventually arrived in 1864 and found their way blocked by the dam, they bombarded the fort out of existence.

Fort Esperanza

An earthwork fortification on the northeastern shore of Matagorda Island, Fort Esperanza was constructed in 1861. A small fort-like emplacement, Fort Washington, dating from 1842 at the southeast corner of the island near a channel lighthouse, had been deemed too exposed to naval gunfire to be effective. Fort Esperanza was built overlooking the Cavallo Pass channel from the Gulf of Mexico into Matagorda Bay, a passage only ten feet deep. The fort sported an impressive number of cannon, eight 24-pounders and one monstrous 128-pounder. The walls of the fort were nine feet high and twenty feet thick.

In October of 1862 a Union fleet forced a passage into Matagorda Bay, the gunners of the fort no match for the cannoneers aboard the Union ships. The Confederates hastily withdrew across the inlet to the town of Indianola on the mainland. After a brief battle there, the town was seized by Union landing parties, and the fleet moved further up the bay to bombard the town of Port Lavaca. But, lacking sufficient ground forces to secure their gains, the Union fleet withdrew from Matagorda Bay in early November. The Confederates reoccupied Indianola and Fort Esperanza.

After the crushing defeat of the Union forces at Fort Griffin in 1863, the focus for an invasion shifted south. Union troops were landed on Matagorda Island, unopposed, in early November and besieged Fort Esperanza. In just two days of heavy fighting, the Confederates realized they were outmanned and outgunned and in danger of being cut off. They evacuated the fort but not before spiking the guns, blowing up the ammunition, and burning their supplies. The victorious Union forces captured nothing of use or value other than the position itself.

The fort was repaired and rearmed, remaining in Federal hands until the spring of 1864. It was then that the troops were withdrawn and sent to Louisiana, allowing the waiting Confederates to once again reclaim their former position. Fort Esperanza would remain under Confederate control until the end of the war and then be abandoned.

Fort Esperanza fell victim to the elements. The eastern walls were destroyed by a coastal storm in 1868, and by 1878 erosion had felled the remaining walls. Today only the remains of a few outlying rifle pits can be barely seen.

Fort Green

In 1861 a sand and log fortification known as Fort Green was erected on the southern end of Bolivar Peninsula, located at the entrance to Galveston Bay north of Galveston Island. But the fort, built largely with slave labor, was in no position to be of any help when Union forces plowed right through into the bay and captured the town of Galveston in 1862. A foraging party sent to the peninsula was repulsed with the aid of Confederate cavalry, and several prisoners were detained at Fort Green. At war's end the post was abandoned.

Later History

When the Federal government purchased ninety-seven acres of land on the Bolivar Peninsula in 1898, all trace of Fort Green was gone. The city of Port Bolivar now occupied the area.

Construction began on a new fort to help guard Galveston Bay; this was the second installation in Texas history to bear the name Fort Travis. Fort Travis was heavily damaged in the great Galveston hurricane of 1900, but a seventeen-foot seawall was added in 1906 to protect the post from any future damage, and reconstruction proceeded. Four separate artillery batteries would eventually defend the fort that consisted of twenty-seven buildings.

Fort Travis was manned during World War I and II, the last artillery battery actually being installed in 1943. German P.O.W.s were also confined at the fort. In 1949 the government sold the site to private interests as surplus inventory. In 1973 the land was acquired by Galveston County and converted into a public park. The buildings were all gone, but the underground fortifications remained and were designated official civil-defense shelters for local residents in case of emergency.

U.S. Army Period (1866-Present)

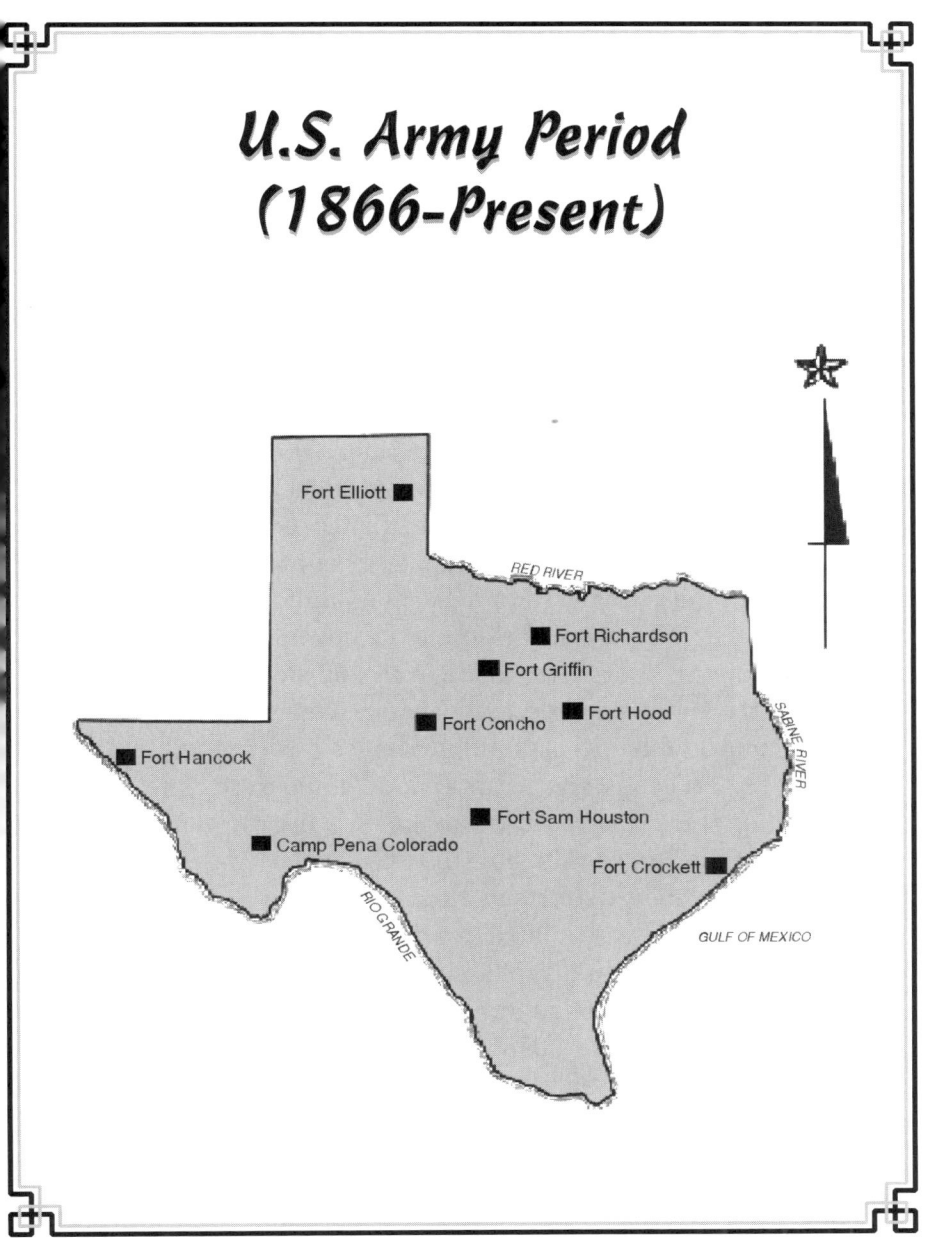

After the Civil War the federal government established a line of forts in Texas to protect civilians on the frontier. The northernmost of these posts was not in operation for long—only eleven years—but its effectiveness was paramount to the western expansion of the day.

Fort Richardson

Enduring a few fitful starts and failures in the area, Fort Richardson was established in 1867 near the site of a stagecoach way station and the small town of Jacksboro. Situated on the south bank of Lost Creek, the first structures of the fort complex were log houses of simple, upright construction. A trench outline was dug, and logs cut to uniform length were put in place, in stockade fashion, to form walls. Roofs were of logs or canvas; doors were made from salvaged lumber. These crude structures were occupied while work went ahead on more comfortable, permanent buildings.

By 1870 a sandstone hospital and commissary were completed, as were five wood frame officers quarters, a bakery, and the guardhouse. The enlisted men still occupied the log buildings as they performed their military duties and provided the construction labor force building the installation. Fort Richardson would probably have remained just another fort of the line had not an incident occurred that would link it to one of the most famous soldiers in U.S. military history.

In 1871 Commanding General William Tecumseh Sherman, veteran of the Civil War, decided to tour the Texas frontier forts to determine if the reported Indian dangers there were, in fact, true. Since he believed the reports to be exaggerated, Sherman traveled with only a small cavalry escort. Eight miles west of Fort Richardson, Sherman's party rode through an Indian ambush site. The warriors, for reasons unknown, allowed the small detachment to pass by unmolested and fell upon the next group to come along, a wagon train of supplies. Sherman learned of the annihilation of the supply train and his near miss after arriving at Fort Richardson. He decided that the reported Indian threat was not overblown and ordered an extended campaign against the local Kiowa and Comanche. Years of sporadic warfare followed.

Two battalions of the 4th Cavalry out of Fort Richardson finally eliminated the Comanche and Kiowa threat in 1874 at the battle of Palo Duro Canyon. This engagement in the Texas Panhandle region brought relative peace, and four years later the fort was of no further use. Fort Richardson was abandoned in 1878.

Later History

By the 1930s the ruins of Fort Richardson had become an eyesore. Citizens of the town of Jacksboro initiated a cleanup program of the facility that restored many of the existing structures to their former appearance. Seven of the post's original buildings were restored and two were reconstructed; the rest were demolished.

There exists today the hospital (now a museum), the commissary, the morgue, a bakery, the powder magazine, part of the guardhouse, one officers quarters, and two enlisted men barracks. An interpretive center, located in the officers quarters, is open daily from 8 A.M. to 5 P.M. and offers exhibits about the history of the fort. Admission is charged.

Fort Richardson State Historical Park is located one mile southeast of Jacksboro on U.S. 281.

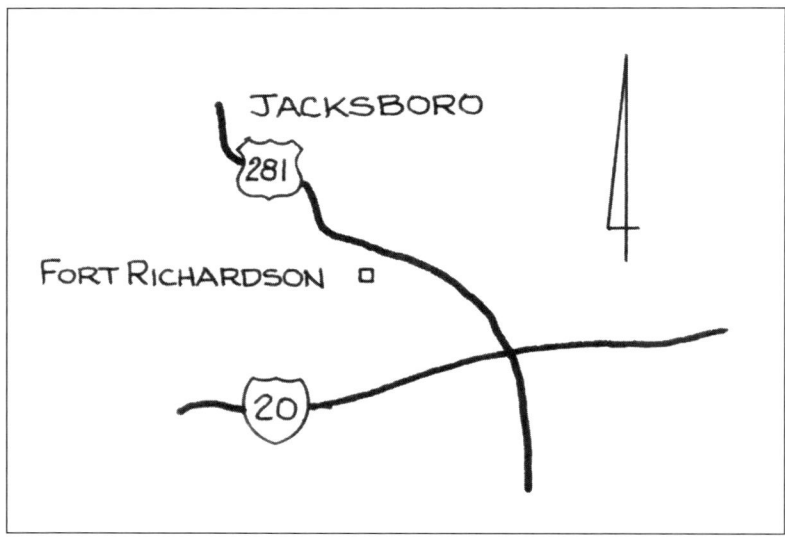

U.S. Army Period (1866-Present)

As the frontier of Texas marched westward and the territory ruled by the Indians shrank, one fort became a focal point in the army's protective line. It was the center of a line of forts that stretched from the northeastern border of Texas to El Paso in the west and also the northernmost post in a line that would run south to the mouth of the Rio Grande.

Fort Concho

One of the few army forts that was not named after a current or deceased military man, Fort Concho was established in 1867 at the junction of the North and Middle Concho Rivers. Its central location in the defensive line of forts necessitated the construction of buildings that would last. Skilled civilian craftsmen from Fredericksburg erected structures of native sandstone on pecan wood framing. Fort Concho would serve as regimental headquarters for the 4th and 10th Cavalry and the 11th and 16th Infantry during its existence. Additionally, units of the 3rd, 8th, and 9th Cavalry would, at various times throughout the fort's twenty-one-year tenure, be stationed there, as would units of the 17th, 19th, 24th, and 25th Infantry.

Fort Concho was strategically located on the El Paso-San Antonio Road where it intersected with the Butterfield Stage route and the Goodnight-Loving cattle trail. This site offered a freedom of movement for the troops garrisoned there that allowed for rapid deployment. Whether the need was to protect civilians or campaign against hostiles, Fort Concho could provide what was required very quickly.

Between 1871 and 1875 the 4th Cavalry mounted active campaigns against the Kiowa, Comanche, and Cheyenne in northwestern Texas. Troops from Fort Concho engaged the

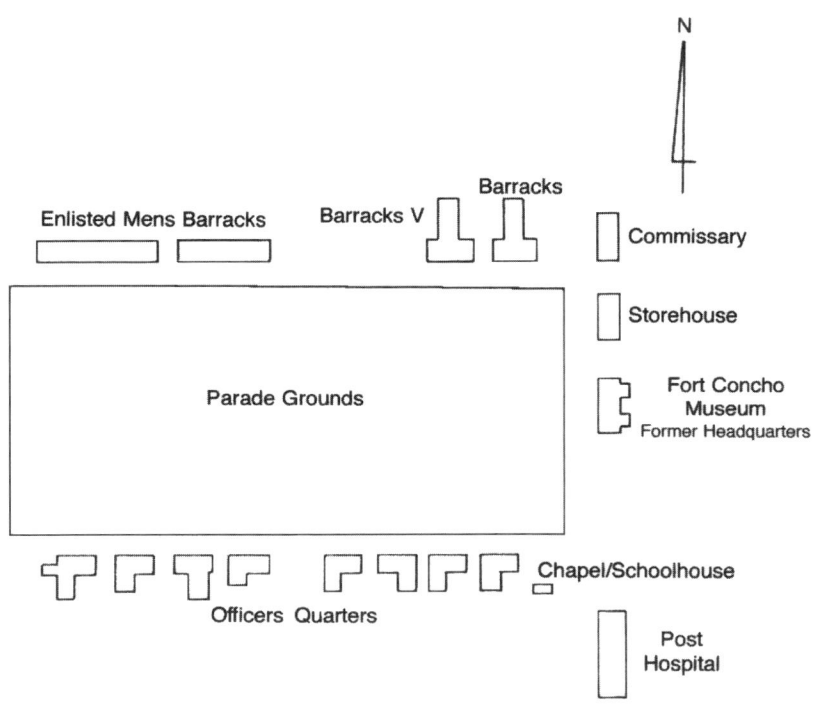

Fort Concho
National Historic Landmark

Indians at the battles of Blanco Canyon in 1871 and Palo Duro Canyon in 1874, actions that led to the withdrawal of hostile tribes from those areas. They also fought the Kickapoo in southwestern Texas and even in northern Mexico when the need arose. The aggressive pursuit of hostiles carried out from Fort Concho was instrumental in pushing the frontier of white settlement ever westward in the 1870s and '80s. By 1889 the fort had outlived its usefulness and was abandoned by the Army in that year.

U.S. Army Period (1866-Present)

Civilians from the nearby town of San Angelo immediately took over the post, converting the thirty or so structures into commercial storage facilities and personal housing. This timely action saved most of the fort's buildings from suffering the ravages of neglect.

Later History

Through the efforts of Ginevra Wood Carson in 1929, a successful fund-raising campaign led to the purchase of the former headquarters building, and the Fort Concho Museum was opened to the public the next year. The city of San Angelo began to acquire other buildings on the site, and by the 1950s two barracks and two mess halls had been rebuilt from the ground up. This civic involvement in the preservation of the fort was rewarded in 1961 when Fort Concho was listed as a national historic landmark by the federal government.

Today the Fort Concho site includes some sixteen original and five reconstructed buildings from the old fort, as well as other historic structures, all in a forty-acre park setting. The museum features exhibits about the fort's history during the Indian Wars, and one enlisted mans barracks (Barracks V) contains a living history display of enlisted mans personal items and equipment maintained by reenactors portraying members of Company D of the 4th Cavalry. This volunteer unit regularly takes part in mounted ceremonies and demonstrations at Fort Concho as well as parades and special events in San Angelo. Fort Concho, like Fort Davis, claims the title of the most exact representation of a frontier fort in the Southwest. A visitor to both facilities would be hard-pressed to make a decision as to which holds the top spot.

Fort Concho National Historic Landmark is located just east of South Oakes Street on East Avenue D in San Angelo.

The museum is open Tuesday through Saturday from 10 A.M. to 5 P.M. and Sunday from 1 P.M. to 5 P.M. It is closed on Thanksgiving, Christmas, and New Year's. Special events are scheduled throughout the year. Admission is charged.

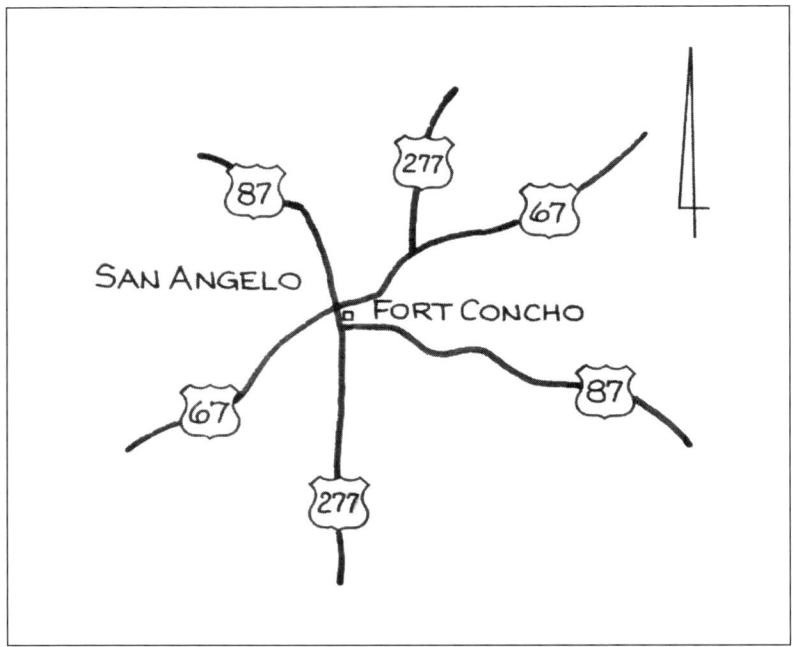

U.S. Army Period (1866-Present)

Fort Griffin

Built on a plateau overlooking the floodplain of the Clear Fork of the Brazos River in 1867, the installation was first named Camp Wilson. Renamed Fort Griffin in 1868, the fort served as a supply depot and staging area for campaigns against the Indians in the Texas Panhandle. Originally constructed of logs, only five buildings of the post were ever rebuilt of stone, and many soldiers quartered there lived in tents. There were at least forty small timber huts designed to hold four men apiece. Each hut measured eight and a half feet by thirteen feet and had two windows, a door, and a fireplace.

The nearby town of Fort Griffin was the main source of social activity for the soldiers, soon earning the reputation as a lawless den of vice and the nickname "The Flat" because it was located below the high ground the fort occupied. The town became a hub of activity in the 1870s with the influx of buffalo hunters into the region. More than 200,000 buffalo hides were shipped back East during the town's heyday. At one time, to cater to the rough tastes of buffalo hunters and soldiers, the town of Fort Griffin boasted several dance halls, at least ten saloons, and many houses of prostitution. It was a wild and dangerous place; thirty-four killings took place there in a twelve-year period. In 1877 no less than two dozen Texas Rangers were assigned to Fort Griffin to keep the peace.

By 1879 the buffalo hunters had virtually wiped out the southern buffalo herds, and the war against the Indians in the Panhandle drew to a successful conclusion. Both the post and town of Fort Griffin had outlived their usefulness. In 1881 the fort was abandoned, the troopers being reassigned to Fort Clark to the south, and the mass exodus from the town that followed turned both sites into empty shells.

Later History

The state of Texas was deeded 506 acres of land, including the fort site, by Shackelford County in 1935. Fort Griffin State Historical Park was opened to the public in 1938, after the ruins of Fort Griffin were inspected and partially restored.

The five original stone buildings stand in ruins, all but one roofless, including the powder magazine, administrative building, bakery, a store, and a structure of unknown usage.

U.S. Army Period (1866-Present)

Partially restored buildings include a mess hall and the hospital. Replicas of the small huts the enlisted men used have been constructed. Many existing stone foundations were uncovered in a 1969 excavation, including an officers and first sergeants quarters. The former town site does not lie within the park boundary.

Fort Griffin State Historical Park is now home to a portion of the official Texas longhorn herd and is located fifteen miles north of Albany on U.S. 283. A visitors center at the park is open daily from 8 A.M. to 5 P.M.

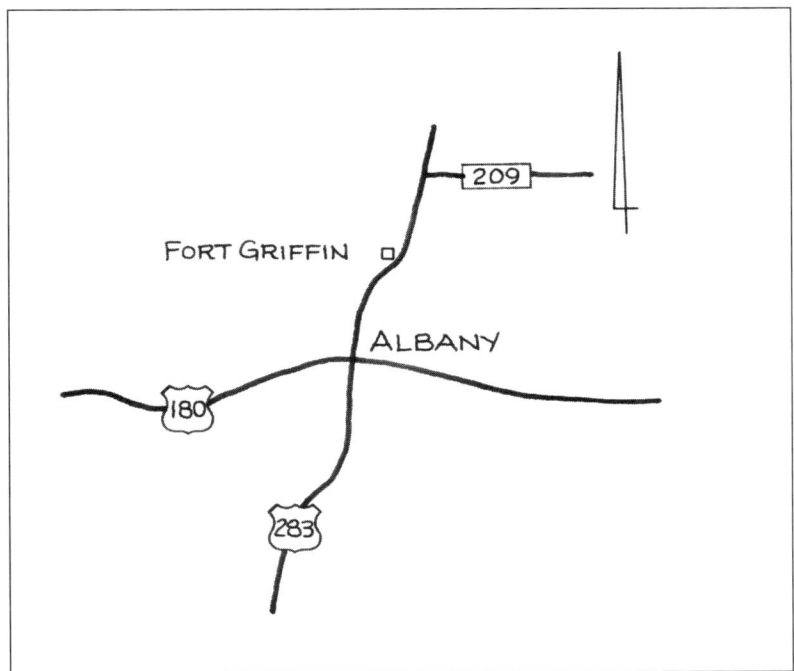

Fort Elliott

This site was established on a low plateau overlooking Sweetwater Creek in 1875 as an advanced outpost in the Texas Panhandle. By 1878 a post commanders home, six officers quarters, a hospital, a post headquarters, five company-size barracks, and a combination school and chapel had been built of lumber brought in from Dodge City. Additionally, a guardhouse, stables, and storehouses were built of cottonwood logs and adobe. In 1879 the headquarters building burned down, but it was immediately rebuilt.

The primary responsibility of Fort Elliott was to guard the borders of Indian Territory (present-day Oklahoma), protect local settlements, and oversee the passage of cattle drives

U.S. Army Period (1866-Present)

headed to Kansas. A company of black troopers of the 10th Cavalry was assigned to the fort in 1879, and other black units would soon follow. By 1884 Fort Elliott was totally a "buffalo soldier" fort, with units of the 24th Infantry and 9th Cavalry stationed there.

In 1887 the first railroad built into the Panhandle bypassed Fort Elliott to the north, virtually assuring its eventual closure. When a typhoid epidemic broke out in 1890, the issue was settled. The fort was abandoned and the buildings and land sold off to private interests. Nothing remains of Fort Elliott today.

One of the largest military installations in Texas started out as a mere quartermasters depot housed in the ruins of the Alamo. Established on a forty-acre tract of land northeast of San Antonio, it has grown over the years to encompass 35,000 acres, or fifty-four square miles.

Fort Sam Houston

Construction began in June of 1876 on a donated parcel of land known as Government Hill. Designed in the shape of a quadrangle, the immense first structure of the fort measured 624 feet along the north wall and 500 feet along the east and west walls. The two-story south wall, the same length as the north, contained the only gate. Inside the gray limestone structure were built houses, offices, and sheds, the exterior walls of the enclosure serving as the rear walls of each building, creating a large central courtyard. In 1877 a ninety-foot tall, fifteen-foot square watchtower was built of limestone to provide a lookout over the surrounding countryside. When completed in 1879, the fort was already occupied by the garrison from San Antonio.

Expansion of the fort began again almost immediately with the addition of officers quarters, a post commanders house, and a temporary hospital. Over the coming years a flurry of building activity would take place, branching out on all sides of the original quadrangle and watchtower. Between 1885 and 1891, forty-three more acres would be added to the fort and sixty buildings were erected, the first being a permanent hospital.

In 1886 a rectangular shaped two-story infantry headquarters building was constructed of yellow brick. Additionally, infantry officers quarters were erected between 1886 and 1889, two-story L-shaped brick buildings with two-tiered verandas along the front and one side. Between 1885 and 1891, infantry barracks for the enlisted men were constructed, each a two-story rectangular shaped building of yellow brick. The infantry barracks buildings formed a "U" shape at the east end of the infantry compound, and in the center of the U stood a three-story guardhouse.

By 1890 the post was officially designated as Fort Sam Houston and continued to grow with the addition of new military units. Each successive spurt of building activity created housing and space for different branches of the army stationed at the fort. An infantry regiment, a cavalry regiment, two artillery batteries, a unit of signal corps, and a unit of engineers were all stationed at Fort Sam Houston, and each occupied a separate installation from the others. Each installation was tied together with its neighbors to create a whole. It did seem that Fort Sam Houston would never be completed.

In 1910 the hospital was expanded to provide 1,000 additional beds. In that same year, the army's very first airplane was brought to the fort, where the pilot received flying lessons through the mail by corresponding with the Wright brothers. The pilot, Lt. Benjamin Foulois, flew the first military flight in U.S. history at Fort Sam Houston. During a public demonstration of the new airplane on March 2, 1910, Foulois delighted the assembled crowd with four flights that included three takeoffs and landings and one takeoff and a crash. The aviation program at Fort Sam Houston was immediately suspended.

But by 1917 the aviation program was back in place and supplying nine airplanes and fifteen pilots to Gen. John J. Pershing to aid in his pursuit of the bandit Pancho Villa through northern Mexico. Fort Sam Houston served as a vital supply depot for Pershing's historic, yet fruitless, incursion. During World War I another 1,280 acres of land was added to the fort that became a staging area for troops on their way to France. By 1928 some 500 more buildings had been constructed.

At the onset of World War II, Fort Sam Houston was the largest army post in the United States and the headquarters of the Southern Defense Command. It served as the largest prisoner of war camp in the country. In 1949, when it was named Fourth United States Army Headquarters, Fort Sam Houston covered over 3,000 acres of land and had 1,500 buildings. During the Korean War, the fort became a major training center for the Army Medical Field Service School.

Later History

Fort Sam Houston is still an active army installation. It is headquarters for not only the Fifth United States Army but also the 902nd Military Intelligence Group, the Joint Military Readiness Center, the Health Services Command, Brooke

Army Medical Center, the Academy of Health Services, the Institute of Surgical Research, and the Army Dental Laboratory. Additionally, the Army Corp of Engineers and West Point Admissions Office are based at the fort. Fort Sam Houston supports all of the Army Reserve and National Guard units in the state of Texas.

The fort itself is a living museum; each building project in its history remains intact and functional. Besides the original Quadrangle, the Staff Post, the Infantry Post, the Cavalry Post, and the Artillery Post cover about 400 acres and contain 130 major historic buildings. A partial listing of the structures would include the Quadrangle, the Watchtower, Infantry Post Headquarters and Officers Quarters, the Infantry Barracks and Bell Tower, the Post Commanders Home, the Artillery Post Officers Quarters, and Old Staff Post Hospital.

The Fort Sam Houston Museum is located in a rectangular shaped two-story building that was once part of the Infantry Post and dates back to 1888. Exhibits there chronicle the growth of Fort Sam Houston from the garrison's occupation of the Alamo in 1845 to the present. Featured are uniforms and equipment, historic events, and profiles of distinguished military leaders who once served at the post, such as John J. Pershing and Dwight D. Eisenhower. The museum is open Wednesday through Sunday from 10 A.M. to 4 P.M. and can provide maps for a self-guided tour of the historic sites on post. The museum is located on Stanley Road.

U.S. Army Period (1866-Present)

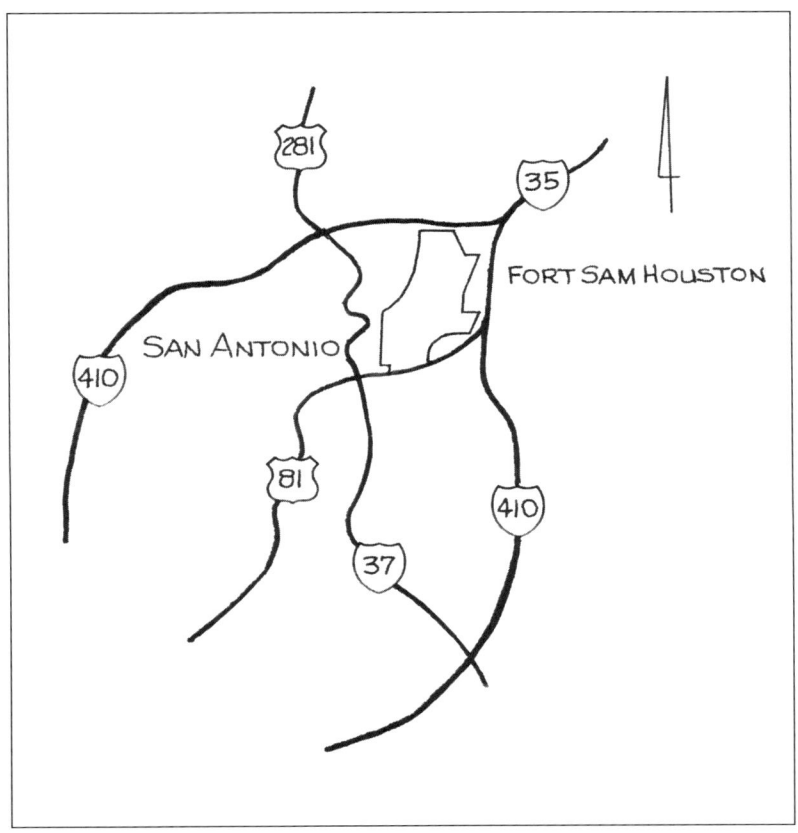

The U.S. Army was not the only military force to require posts in Texas to operate from. In the latter part of the nineteenth century the forerunner of the Texas National Guard needed a base.

Camp Mabry

Established in 1892 on an eighty-five-acre site three miles northwest of Austin, Camp Mabry was originally home of the Texas Volunteer Guard. By 1909 the federal government had purchased and donated to the state an additional two hundred acres for use as training grounds for the guardsmen. More acreage was donated by local property owners to increase the size of the camp to four hundred acres by 1911.

During the Spanish-American War, Camp Mabry was utilized as a mobilization site for troops on their way to Cuba. The State Arsenal was moved to the camp from downtown Austin in 1915, and during World War I the U.S. Army used the post as a training site, erecting several new barracks and administration buildings. When the Texas National Guard was called into service during World War II, the State Militia was headquartered at Camp Mabry until the regular guardsmen returned from overseas. In the early 1950s the camp was the chief training facility for the Department of Public Safety and the Texas Rangers. By 1959 the Texas National Guard State Officer Candidate School had been established at the camp.

Later History

In 1992 Camp Mabry celebrated its 100th year of operation. By that time the post was the home of the Texas National Guard Academy, opened in 1984. The camp was also

U.S. Army Period (1866-Present)

headquarters for the Texas State Guard, the Texas Air National Guard, the headquarters armory for the 49th Armored Division, and the United States Property and Fiscal Management Office.

The camp today also houses the Texas Military Forces Museum. The museum is located in Building 6 at 2200 West 35th Street. Exhibits, dioramas, and archives cover the history of the Texas military from the Texas Revolution through Desert Storm. The hours of operation are Wednesday through Sunday from 10 A.M. to 4 P.M.

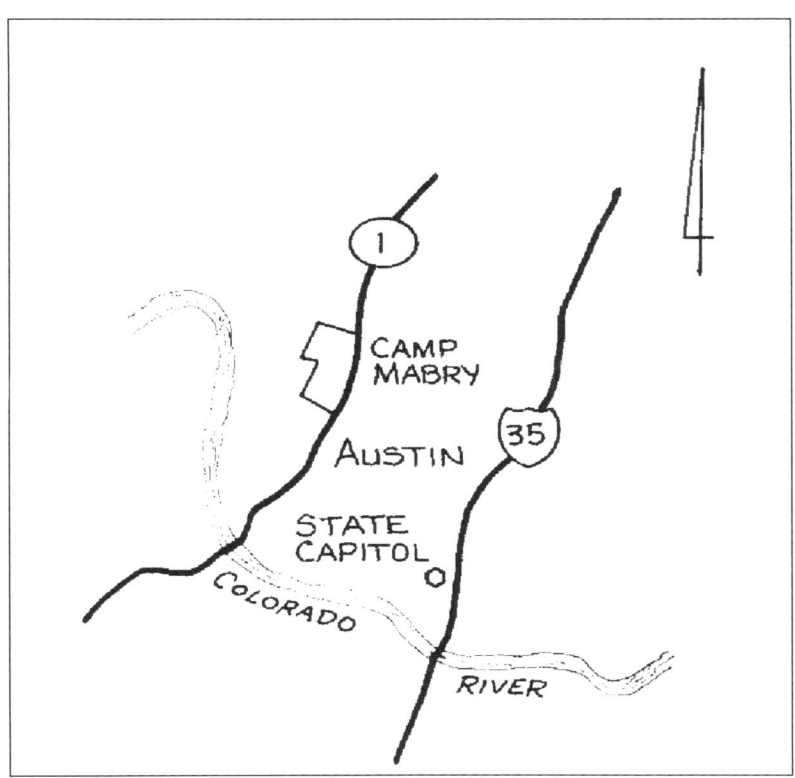

Fort Crockett

Fort Crockett was built on Galveston Island in 1897 as an artillery training facility and harbor defense. The fort's batteries of ten-inch guns and mortars were strategically positioned to cover any approach from the Gulf of Mexico. Fort Crockett suffered severe damage in the great hurricane of 1900, and in 1904-5 a seawall was constructed that tied into the concrete gun emplacements along the ocean. This work was done by the Army Corps of Engineers, who were caretakers for the installation until it was regarrisoned by regular troops in 1911.

Fort Crockett served as headquarters for the 69th Coast Artillery from 1917 to 1926. In the mid-1920s an aerodrome was built nearby. In 1941 the 20th and 265th Coast Artillery units manned the fixed battery positions. German prisoners of war were interned at the fort during World War II. After the war Fort Crockett served as recreational facility for active duty and reserve military men and their families.

U.S. Army Period (1866-Present)

By 1955 the government began selling off the property and buildings to Galveston College, Texas A&M University at Galveston, and the National Marine Fisheries Service. The coastal artillery bunkers can still be seen, many becoming the foundation for a hotel and conference center. The remains of Fort Crockett are located on Seawall Boulevard, between 45th and 53rd Streets.

Fort San Jacinto

Constructed on the eastern end of Galveston Island in 1898, the fort's three gun batteries were mounted behind a seventeen-foot seawall fronting the Gulf of Mexico. The fort was the first headquarters for Galveston's harbor defense system from 1918 to 1926. After World War II the installation was turned over to the U.S. Coast Guard and housed an electronics repair facility. In 1986 the site was transferred to the Army Corps of Engineers for use as a base during dredging operations in the Galveston Ship Channel.

Fort D.A. Russell

In 1911, with Mexico in the throes of yet another revolution, Texas border towns were vulnerable to raids by any of the warring factions. To counter this threat, U.S. Cavalry troops were sent to establish an installation near the town of Marfa. The post was first named Camp Albert and served as the main base for army biplanes flying patrols along the Rio Grande. Renamed Camp Marfa, the post was garrisoned by troops rotated in and out from Fort Bliss in El Paso.

During World War I the post was expanded and was soon designated as headquarters of the Marfa command sector. In 1923 simulated combat maneuvers were first held there, and in 1930 the name was changed, for the third time, to Fort D.A. Russell. In 1933 the fort was deactivated, the troops reassigned, and a skeleton garrison left behind to maintain the buildings.

By 1935 the fort was regarrisoned by the 77th Field Artillery. With World War II came an expansion of 2,400 acres of land donated by civilian property owners, and over 1,000 men were stationed at the post. During the war a prisoner of war camp was established at the fort.

Fort D.A. Russell was deactivated again in 1945 and officially closed in 1946. By 1949 most of the lands and buildings of the fort had been sold off to private citizens.

U.S. Army Period (1866-Present)

Fort Hood

With the United States entry into World War II, a tank destroyer tactical and firing center was established near Killeen in January of 1942. Units from all over the country arrived at such a rapid rate that the facility expanded quickly, swallowing up over 300 farms and ranches in the vicinity for immediate use as training grounds. As the war progressed Camp Hood, as it was known then, began to train tank and armored infantry units. Over 100,000 men were trained for combat during World War II. By the end of the war, more than 4,000 German prisoners of war were being held there. Officially named Fort Hood in 1950, the facility had grown by almost 50,000 acres by 1953.

Throughout the remainder of the twentieth century, Fort Hood provided the training in armored combat necessary for the United States military to engage in such conflicts as Korea, Vietnam, and in Iraq during Desert Storm. Fort Hood over the years has served as home base for such units as the 1st, 2nd, and 4th Armored Divisions and the 5th United States Army.

Today Fort Hood is the largest active military installation in the free world, covering over 339 square miles. It is the only two-division post in the nation, home to the 1st Cavalry Division and the 4th Infantry Division. Both divisions maintain their own museums on post.

The 1st Cavalry Division Museum chronicles over 150 years of U.S. Cavalry history, from the boots-and-saddles period to tank warfare. Exhibits include everything from sabers to attack helicopters.

The 4th Infantry Division Museum presents the history of the division with photographs, text, and artifacts.

Both museums are open to the public Mondays through Fridays from 9 A.M. to 3:30 P.M. and weekends from noon to 3:30 P.M. They are closed on New Year's Day, Easter, Thanksgiving, and Christmas. Located at Fort Hood in Killeen, just off U.S. 190, the museums are accessed through the Main Gate.

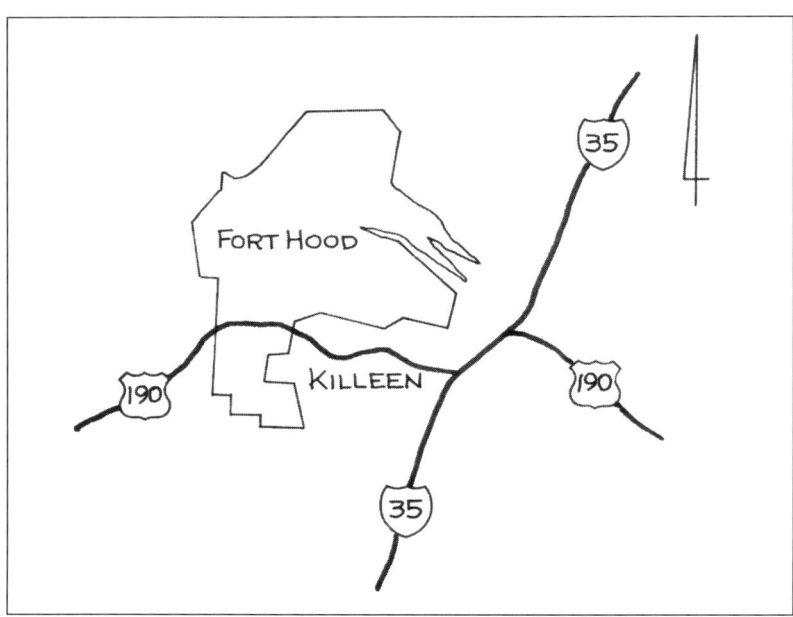

Bibliography

Books

America's Historic Places. Pleasantville, New York: Readers Digest Association, 1988.

Fehrenbach, T. R. *Lone Star: A History of Texas and the Texans.* New York, New York: Wing Books, 1968.

Groneman, Bill. *Battlefields of Texas.* Plano, Texas: Republic of Texas Press, 1998.

_____. *Eyewitness to the Alamo.* Plano, Texas: Republic of Texas Press, 1996.

Hardin, Stephen L. *Texian Iliad: A Military History of the Texas Revolution.* Austin, Texas: University of Texas Press, 1994.

Hopewell, Clifford. *Remember Goliad: Their Silent Tents.* Austin, Texas: Eakin Press, 1998.

Nelson, George. *The Alamo: An Illustrated History.* Uvalde, Texas: Aldine Press, 1998.

Pool, William C. *A Historical Atlas of Texas.* Austin, Texas: Encino Press, 1975.

Reynolds, Lindor. *Forts & Battlefields of the Old West.* New York, New York: M & M Books, 1991.

The Soldiers, The Mexican War, The Spanish West. New York, New York: Time-Life Books, 1976.

Wooster, Robert. *Soldiers, Sutlers and Settlers: Garrison Life on the Texas Frontier.* College Station, Texas: Texas A&M University Press, 1987.

_____. *Texas and Texans in the Civil War.* Austin, Texas: Eakin Press, 1995.

Bibliography

Periodicals

Southwestern Historical Quarterly, Texas State Historical Association, Austin, Texas

    Coker, Caleb and Janent G. Humphrey, "The Texas Frontier in 1850: Dr. Ebenezer Swift and the view from Fort Martin Scott," Jan. 1993, Vol. XCVI, No. 3

    Smith, Thomas T., "Fort Inge and Texas Frontier Military Operations 1849-1869," July 1992, Vol. XCVI, No. 1

Wild West, Empire Press, Leesburg, Virginia

    Brockway, Michael D., "Fort Martin Scott," June 1993, Vol. 6, No. 1

    Deac, Wilfred P., "Victory By A Longshot," Dec. 1989, Vol. 2, No. 4

    Dettman, Bruce and Michael Bedford, "Prisoners Shown No Mercy," Dec. 1990, Vol. 3, No. 4

    McDaniel, Reginald E., "Buffalo Soldiers Won Their Spurs," Feb. 1995, Vol. 7, No. 5

    Smith, Robert Barr, "Biggest Indian Fight," April 1992, Vol. 4, No. 6

    Wilkins, Frederick, "The Texas Rangers: Birth And Legend," Aug. 1998, Vol. 11, No. 2

    Wukovits, John F., "Vision Pursued Tenaciously," Oct. 1990, Vol. 3, No. 3

Texas Highways, Texas Department of Transportation, Austin, Texas

    Baumgardner, Robert, "Menard's Mettle," June 1994, Vol. 41, No. 6

    Boyd, Eva Jolene, "Historic Fort Stockton," Nov. 1994, Vol. 41, No. 11

    Cox, Mike, "The Comanche War Trail: Terror in the Night," Aug. 1997, Vol. 44, No. 8

    Edwards, Janet R., "Fort Clark Springs: Splash into the Past," May 1999, Vol. 46, No. 5

Fowler, Gene, "Maverick Town Eagle Pass," Feb. 1997, Vol. 44, No. 2

Longoria, Arturo, "Fabled Fort Ringgold," Jan. 1993, Vol. 40, No. 1

Morrison, Dan, "Cibolo Creek Ranch," Nov. 1999, Vol. 46, No. 11

Myers, Cindi, "Presidio La Bahia: Goliad's Historic Citadel," Mar. 1999, Vol. 46, No. 3

Smith-Rodgers, Sheryl, "Gusto On The Concho," Dec. 1997, Vol. 44, No. 12

Online Resources

Texas Historical Commission, Texas Historic Sites Atlas, atlas.thc.state.tx.us

Texas State Travel Guide 2000, Texas Dept. of Transportation, Travel Division, Austin, Texas

Texas Parks & Wildlife, www.tpwd.state.tx.us

Texas State Historical Association & Center for Studies in Texas History, Handbook of Texas Online, www.tsha.utexas.edu

Texas State Library and Archives Commission, www.tsl.state.tx.us

Texas Military Forces Museum, www.kwanah.com/txmilmus

Brochures and Pamphlets

Abilene, Texas
Abilene Convention & Visitors Bureau
Abilene Visitor's Guide & Map

Fort Clark Springs, Inc.
Fort Clark Springs

Bibliography

City of San Angelo, Texas
Fort Concho National Historic Landmark

Fort Davis, Texas
Fort Davis Chamber of Commerce

City of Killeen, Texas
Fort Hood Museums

Fort Stockton, Texas
Fort Stockton—Your Crossroads to Adventure
Historic Fort Stockton

Fort Worth, Texas
Fort Worth Convention & Visitors Bureau
Fort Worth Official Visitor's Guide
Texas Historical Commission
Texas Forts Trail
Texas in the Civil War

Texas Parks & Wildlife
Fort Griffin
Fort Lancaster
Fort Leaton
Fort McKavett
Fort Parker
Old Fort Parker
Fort Richardson
Sabine Pass Battleground

National Park Service
Palo Alto Battlefield—Fort Brown
Fort Davis

Index

A
Adobe Walls, 81-87
Alamo, 10-20
Apaches, 120, 122
Army forts, 106-108

B
Barbier, Gabriel Minime Sieur, 5
Battle of Adobe Walls, 83-87
Battle of Sabine Pass, 191, 193
Battles of the Alamo, 11-15
black soldiers, 156-157, 170-173
Blair's Fort, 181
Bowie, James, 48
Bowie, Rezin, 48
Bradburn, Juan, 52-54
Brazoria, 58
Brown, Major Jacob, 98-99
buffalo hunters, 84, 209
buffalo soldiers, 154, 158, 170, 213
Buffalo Springs, 109, 190

C
camels, 160-161
Camp Bowie, 88
Camp Breckenridge, 178
Camp Chambers, 89
Camp Collier, 178
Camp Cooper, 163-164
Camp Crockett, 89
Camp Cureton, 178
Camp Dix, 135, 179
Camp Ford, 182-184
Camp Houston, 112
Camp Mabry, 218-219
Camp McMillan, 179
Camp Montel, 179
Camp Nueces, 179
Camp Pecan, 179
Camp Pena Colorado, 110
Camp Rabb, 180
Camp Ringgold, 114
Camp Salmon, 180
Camp San Saba, 180
Camp Semmes, 196
Camp Verde, 160-161, 180
Camp Wood, 109
Carson, Col. Christopher (Kit), 83
Cibolo Creek Ranch, 168
Collinsworth, 27
Comanche, 45-47, 68, 70, 83-84, 112, 141
Cos, Gen. Martin Perfecto de, 11

D
Daughters of the Republic of Texas (DRT), 17
Davis Family Fort, 188
Dixon, Billy, 86

E
East Tejas presidios, 41
Edwards, Haden, 38

Index

El Fortin de Cienega, 166
El Fortin del Cibolo, 166-168
El Fortin la Morita, 166
Espriella, Pedro, 41

F

family forts, 76, 187
Fannin, Col. James W., 28, 30-32
Faver, Milton, 166-167
Fort Adobe, 81
Fort Anahuac, 52-55
Fort Belknap, 137-140
Fort Bend, 66-67
Fort Bird, 87
Fort Bliss, 120-124
Fort Brown, 100-101
Fort Burleson, 90-92
Fort Chadbourne, 150
Fort Cibolo, 166
Fort Clark, 146-149
Fort Coleman, 93
Fort Colorado, 93
Fort Concho, 205-208
Fort Crockett, 220-221
Fort Croghan, 126
Fort D.A. Russell, 222
Fort Davis, 154-159, 166-167, 187
Fort Defiance, 28-31
Fort Duncan, 128-130
Fort Elliott, 212-213
Fort Esperanza, 197-198
Fort Ewell, 110
Fort Fisher, 78-79
Fort Gates, 108
Fort Goliad, 26
Fort Graham, 108

Fort Green, 198
Fort Griffin, 191-194, 209-211
Fort Grigsby, 195
Fort Hancock, 110-111
Fort Hood, 223-224
Fort Houston, 72
Fort Hudson, 164-165
Fort Inge, 135
Fort Lacy, 71
Fort Lancaster, 162
Fort Leaton, 117-118
Fort Lincoln, 108
Fort Lipantitlan, 61-63
Fort Lyday, 77
Fort Manhassett, 195
Fort Marcy, 96
Fort Martin Scott, 112-113
Fort Mason, 144-145
Fort McIntosh, 131-133
Fort McKavett, 151-153
Fort Merrill, 109
Fort Milam, 73, 90
Fort Oldham, 78
Fort Parker, 68-70
Fort Phantom Hill, 141-142
Fort Picketville, 154
Fort Polk, 103
Fort Quintana, 196
Fort Quitman, 175-176
Fort Richardson, 202-204
Fort Ringgold, 114-116
Fort Sabine, 189-190
Fort Sam Houston, 16, 213-216
Fort San Jacinto, 221
Fort Sherman, 89
Fort St. Louis, 4-6, 23
Fort Stockton, 170-174

Fort Tenoxtitlan, 64-65
Fort Teran, 66
Fort Terrett, 109
Fort Texas, 97
Fort Travis, 88, 198-199
Fort Velasco, 57-60
Fort Waul, 155-186
Fort Worth, 125-126
Foulois, Lt. Benjamin, 215
Fuerte de Santa Cruz del Cibolo, 34

G
Goliad, 30
Gonzales, 11

H
Hart's Mill, 120, 122
Houston, Sam, 67
Kickapoo, 150
Kiowa, 83-84

L
Lacy, Martin, 71
Lafitte, Jean, 38
LaSalle, Rene Robert Cavelier Sieur de, 4-5
Leaton, Ben, 120
Lee, Robert E., 116, 165
Little River Fort, 90
Long, Dr. James, 26, 37-38

M
Magee-Gutierrez, 25, 37
Matamoros, 97
McCulloch, Sam, 28
McCulloch's Station, 126

N
Nacogdoches, 36, 39

Nuestra Señora de Guadalupe de los Nacogdoches, 36

O
Oldham, William, 78

P
Parker, Cynthia Ann, 70, 164
Parker, Daniel, 68-69
Parker, Quanah, 70, 85, 164
Pershing, Gen. John J., 215
Piedras, Col. Jose de las, 38
Poindexter, John, 168
Presidio de Nuestra Señora de las Caldas de Guajoquilla, 35
Presidio La Bahia, 23-27
Presidio Nuestra Señora de Loreto, 23
Presidio Nuestra Señora de los Dolores de los Tejas, 41
Presidio Nuestra Señora del Pilar de los Adaes, 41
Presidio San Agustin de Ahumada, 44-45
Presidio San Antonio de Bexar, 20-22
Presidio San Elizario, 35
Presidio San Francisco Xavier de Gigedo, 41, 43
Presidio San Luis de las Amarillas, 45
presidios, 2-3

R
Real Presidio de San Saba, 47-49
Red River Station, 180
Ruiz, Lt. Col. Jose Francisco, 64-65

Index

S

San Antonio de Valero, 7-10
San Jacinto, 67
San Saba, 48
Santa Anna, Antonio Lopez de, 10, 14
Seminole-Negro Indian scouts, 147, 149
Sherman, General William Tecumseh, 202-203
Smith, General Persifor F., 96, 154
Spanish Governor's Palace, 22

Stone Fort, 37-40

T

Taylor, General Zachery, 98-99
Texas Ranger Hall of Fame, 79
Texas Rangers, 73, 77, 79, 90
Travis, William Barret, 54-55
Tumlinson Fort, 72

V

Velasco, 58-59

Y

Y'Barbo House, 36
Y'Barbo, Don Antonio Gil, 36